Blue Monday

Stories of Absurd Realities
and Natural Philosophies

AUDC
Robert Sumrell & Kazys Varnelis

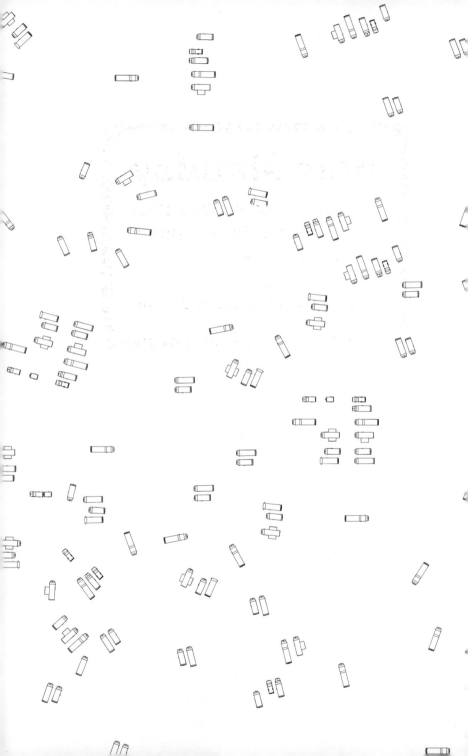

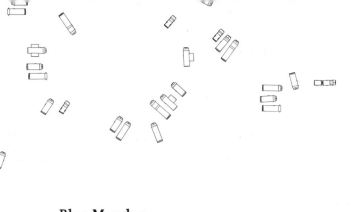

Blue Monday

Peripheral Vision

Reinhold Martin

It is often said that the age of grand narratives is over. In their place are only little stories, or maybe anthologies—collections of little stories. So it is probably not an accident that this book begins with the (knowingly dubious) announcement of the end of the novel. Or more precisely, this book of little stories that are apparently about architecture and urbanism begins by announcing the "end" of fiction as a model of reality, of which the novel is a classic example.

What are we to make of such an announcement? Right or wrong, what does a literary form like the novel have to do with architecture in the first place? Well, there is a sense here that we are in a kind of contemporary twilight zone, where the old cliché of truth being stranger than fiction no longer captures the reality of the world with which architecture and urbanism are confronted. In this collection of not-so-modest little stories by Robert Sumrell and Kazys Varnelis of the formerly-Los Angeles based Architecture Urbanism Design Collaborative (AUDC), what we might call architecture's reality principle—its presumed instrumentality, but also its ongoing capitulation to all sorts of perceived realities, especially of the "late capitalist" variety—is temporarily suspended. In its place are true stories whose subject matter reads like an update of Borges's famous Chinese encyclopedia: lemmings, a woman who married the Berlin wall, Los Angeles's biggest black box, a record collector named Clarence, Muzak, a headless chicken, and Quartzsite, Arizona.

Such a list might lead us to conclude that we are confronted here with a mere diversion, an entertaining interlude to distract us as we take a break from the important business of (say) designing buildings and cities. But surely you remember that someone famous once said that architecture is best perceived in a state of distraction. And surely this *aperçu* applies not only to the peripheral vision of yesterday's *flâneur*, but also to today's surfer, riding the currents of the big city (or in the case of Quartzsite, the temporary town). Right? Well, yes and no, since the surfer and the *flâneur* are not exactly analogous. For the *flâneur*, distraction is everything. While for the surfer it is—in the extreme circumstances of which L. A.'s beaches might not be the best example—death. Or to put it another way, the book you are holding in your hands is not about going with the flow. It is about a kind of resistance, the resistance of "reality" itself.

Nor would the metaphor of "sampling" quite capture the extraordinarily productive strategy mapped out by this book. Since the temporary suspension of architecture's reality principle means that there is not necessarily a self-evident archive of pre-existent facts—objects, texts, techniques, etc.—to sample and remix. Instead, it might be better to think of *Blue Monday* as what its title pretty much says it is: a collection. But it is not exactly a collection of historical anecdotes, of entertaining little stories with no unifying theme. It is, I think, more like a record collection, the logic of which is hinted at by the cover song, released by New Order in 1983.

And if this collection of little stories, little histories, is more like a collection of 12" singles and LPs both grand and obscure, Clarence the record collector holds the key to the whole project. I don't want to give everything away here at the beginning, but suffice it to say that Clarence has a thing for records of all kinds. He is so helpless when confronted with the fast-fading logic of vinyl (what Friedrich Kittler once described as the Real of all media technologies), that he more or less buries himself in it. Sumrell and Varnelis describe collections like Clarence's as aspiring to "an impossibly complete and perfect scale model of the world," a characterization that applies equally well to *Blue Monday*. And of course we are speaking here of both the song and the book—for the perverse (though possibly apocryphal) history of the best-selling 12" single ever is that it lost money, due to the ambitions of its graphic design to simulate a now-obsolete medium of simulation, the floppy disk. You can see where we are going here: from the piles of vinyl in Clarence's kitchen, to the vinyl of

"Blue Monday," to the faux-vinyl, magnetic "floppy" driving media technologies that were still new at the time that Joy Division morphed into New Order.

In a sense all of these imprints are, precisely, recordings. As is *Blue Monday*, a book that records their becoming-obsolete and in the process, their becoming all-consuming and all-powerful. But if you believe that what we have here is a kind of record collection, the question remains: records (or recordings) of what? This brings us back to the beginning, where we noted Varnelis and Sumrell's announcement of the end of fiction as recorded in the novel. Seen from this perspective, the little stories collected here are both real and imaginary at once. That is, they record objects and events that can still be called historical facts. But they do so in a way that puts their reality-value (as distinct from their truth-value) in doubt. In other words, the historical realities recorded here are made to seem imaginary, made up, like some kind of weird architectural project. Who, after all, could have designed the ridiculous urban and mass cultural logistics of a place like Quartzsite (if we can even call it a "place," an architectural term that seems as obsolete as vinyl)? In a similar vein, the believability of the story that records the adventures of Mike the headless chicken rests not so much on the biological oddity of its subject, but on the intimacy with which his owner identified with Mike according to the emotional protocols of the mass media. Call it an allegory of biopolitics, or the politics of life.

There is a way, however, that the subject matter of AUDC's stories still seems to skirt around the subject matter named in the firm's uppercase acronym: Architecture and Urbanism. Or maybe it's the other way around. Maybe these stories are too close to architecture for us to recognize it. After all, reading them we find ourselves literally inside the wiring, or trapped in the elevator. And maybe the resolution is also too high, the focus too precise. Something like this is implied by the sheer beauty of the photographs. Who but architects would bother to photograph a tangle of wires in such a way as to seem to reveal its darkest urban secrets? More than merely forensic, like the jacket design of New Order's "Blue Monday," the many photographs illustrating *Blue Monday* are artful, which is not the same thing as calling them works of art since their job is not to solicit affect, but only its possibility. Just as the New Wave of New Order converted what the authors describe as the authentic emotions of Punk into a kind of scripted consumable, these photographs merely point toward an emotional involvement with their subject while also pointing toward the horizon of its impossibility.

Consider, again, Quartzsite. It scarcely needs to be said that its presentation here owes much to the collections of rocks assembled by the longtime rock collector Robert Smithson in his Site/Non-Site series. But if the artfulness of AUDC's photos seems to "clean up" the rough-and-ready matter-of-factness of

Smithson's documentary style or even (dare we say) to aestheticize its anti-aesthetic, we should not be misled so easily. Retranslated back into architecture, we might instead observe that Quartzsite, presented here as a temporary, pseudo-nomadic market for very heavy, useless objects (stones), gives new meaning to the "strictly architectural" term "local stone." Hardly a thing that anchors this "city" to some metaphysically earthbound "place," local stone is precisely the thing that circulates and, in an allegory of globalization, thereby puts this place—Quartzsite, Arizona—on the map, in circulation.

Both real and imaginary, then, the stories collected in *Blue Monday* are also, like Quartzsite's rocks, strictly useless. They will not tell you how to design a building or lay out a city. But they will help you understand what buildings and cities are, in reality. Yes, reality, as in reality TV, a phenomenon whose actuality is measured in the fantasies that it services, for real. For it seems these days that not enough architects watch enough TV or listen to enough music or read enough stories. Maybe they are too busy with the serious business of designing buildings and cities. Whatever the reason, their diligence in attending to the harsh "realities" of clients and construction seems, all too often, to leave precious little time to understand how these realities are manufactured. That job, it seems, is left for thinkers with time on their hands like AUDC. Which is another way of returning to where we began, for if this collection of little stories seems frivolously to record the exchange of useless rocks and the perambulations of undead chickens, it is because behind and between its episodes there is, in reality, a big story.

Borrowing from others, Varnelis and Sumrell give this big story big names like "Empire" or "late capitalism." Whether or not you accept the nuanced premises that come with these names, you have to admit that the state of affairs they point to is—dare we say it again—far more "real" than the real world of clients and construction. Or better, it is what makes those realities real in the first place. So architecture remains a protagonist in the big story written between the lines of *Blue Monday*.

If Quartzsite, Arizona models the city-as-such as a collection of useless objects, a kind of rock collection, seemingly inert buildings like L. A.'s One Wilshire, modeled and photographed with loving care by AUDC, turn out to be very special rocks indeed. Like the Muzak that once played in elevators and office landscapes from L. A. to New York, One Wilshire is background. "Perhaps the worst building SOM ever designed" (according to the authors), we discover that it harbors the secrets of the information age, material evidence of our becoming-virtual. This is a crucial point and an important contribution that resonates throughout this book: there is nothing immaterial about virtuality. Instead, virtuality is to be understood as another order of materiality, made of cables and connections routed through buildings like this one, but also through every building in both the background and foreground of our collective imagination.

It is similarly bracing, in this age of Disney concert halls, to learn that the cliché of architecture as frozen music, recently renewed in downtown L. A., has in the latter part of the twentieth century been accompanied by the "Stimulus Progression," or the aural management of psychic life materialized in Muzak. Again, these are real things, real theories, and real practices that confirm the importance, for architecture and urbanism, of what you don't quite see, or what you hear only in the background or see only at the periphery of your otherwise too-well-trained vision. So too is there something poignant in the realization that the dynamism of the elevator, once thought to be the very engine driving delirious New York, had already dissolved by mid-century into the anaesthetic haze of "elevator music." Poignant, not because it seems to capture in microcosm the postwar neutralization of modern architecture's mechanical intensity, but because it signals another kind of intensity that architecture and urbanism have only barely begun to grasp.

The intensity in question is that of the intensely banal. It is this intensity that drives the post-urban city, as systematically as the graph of carefully managed environmental stimuli that is the organizing (and organizational) logic of Muzak. AUDC's self-

declared role models, the Italian group Archizoom, attempted
to diagram their own version of the ruthlessly, relentlessly banal
in "negative utopias" of the late 1960s like No-Stop-City.
For Archizoom this intense banality was literally horizontal—
modulated networks stretching into seeming infinite expanses
of what was, essentially, a combination of post-industrial labor
and post-industrial leisure. But there was something a little too
pure, a little too modern about Archizoom's vision of postmoder-
nity as a fluorescent-lit supermarket. Or so it seems when we are
confronted with the careful randomness of AUDC's inventory.
For it is, I think, not only that (as the authors suggest)
Quartzsite, Arizona may be a (mobile) home for the multitude.
It is also that such places offer new sites for Architecture and
Urbanism to rethink their own histories. This kind of rethinking will involve, inevitably and necessarily, a rethinking of modernism's collective project, seemingly canned and packaged for
distribution to individual consumers on the imaginary shelves of
Archizoom's imaginary supermarket, with Muzak playing in the
background. But if it is to be effective, such a rethinking must
occur from within as much as from without—from within the
discipline's center as much as from its peripheries. Or better yet,
it must conjure a state of affairs in which center and periphery
trade places or even cancel each other out.

If you are already thinking "yes—after all, that's the logic of the network model that seems to lie behind all of AUDC's work," you may be right. But there remains the possibility that a truly peripheral vision would not merely replace one center with many centers, or with the dissolution of centrality as such. Nor, for that matter, would it merely replace the monumental verticality of the skyscraper with the horizontal banality of the supermarket. What is hinted at here is, instead, a kind of revolution, where the circularity that defines real, imaginary objects and processes such as those collected in *Blue Monday*, is understood as an end in itself—a model of the world and a map of the battlefield. Think of it like this: the periphery is a product of the center, and Quartzsite is a product of the global city. So to go there is also to go here, to the elevator core of Empire's headquarters. What you will find in such places is not the eccentric, socio-technological or mass cultural residue of Architecture and Urbanism properly understood as the subject of university curricula and professional practices. No, what you will find is something like the operating system of the System itself. Go there with this book as your guide, and you'll see.

REALITY

LEMMINGS

INTRODUCTION

LEMMINGS

Fiction is dead. But don't mourn its passing, the novel—a word literally signifying "the new"—enjoyed a healthy run. Displacing romantic epics as the dominant genre of literature some 250 years ago, novels were a key part of the bourgeois shift toward realism, showing life matter-of-factly instead of according to an ideal vision. Abandoning the classical tradition of forming language according to poetic rules, novelists claimed to craft a transparent window onto the world. Fiction became the means by which the growing middle class learned to construct itself, creating habits and tastes appropriate to life within a bourgeois nation-state.

Today, non-fiction replaces fiction. Biographies, memoirs, histories, and self-help books increasingly dominate the bookstore. Television sitcoms and one-hour dramas give way to 24-hour news, reality television, celebrity biographies, cooking shows, history and science documentaries, as well as an endless stream of pundits. Ours is a world of harrowing real-life drama, how-to decorating shows, impossible-but-true trivia and perpetually happy news. While the novel was fiction's most direct form, documentary film and video are the primary media forms for non-fiction narratives. Just as lyrical epics were collectively created and experienced through endless retellings, novels thrived in the detached meeting of an individual author with an individual subject through the pages of a printed book. Documentary films and videos, on the other hand, deliver an immersive experience of the real, putting the viewer, as much as possible, into the event itself. More than that, documentary films and videos promise the purported traces of the real in the form of light reproduced from film or magnetic tape that were once in turn, exposed to photons reflected by the object of the documentary.

The transparency of the novel was its own most cunning fiction, an artificial construction for putting modernity into an easily comprehensible form. So it is for non-fiction as well. Released in 1924, Robert J. Flaherty's *Nanook of the North* was the first feature-length documentary film. Flaherty spent months living among the Inuit in an attempt to better understand his subject, but in order to make the story of the Eskimos appealing to viewers, he fictionalized many aspects of Nanook and his family's lives, making them seem quainter and more backwards than they really were. When critics learned that Flaherty asked Nanook to hunt using spears as his ancestors did instead of the gun he was accustomed to, they accused him of taking liberties with the truth. Flaherty defended his method, arguing that to catch a thing's true spirit, the filmmaker has to distort it.

Ever since, the barren landscape of the polar regions has attracted documentary filmmakers eager to test their mettle in a reality their audiences will never experience first-hand. The Academy Award winning 1958 documentary *White Wilderness*, part of Disney's *True-Life Adventure* series, returned to the same general location and method pioneered by Flaherty, using animals to make the story of the frozen North less threatening and thereby easier to comprehend. To make the film, nine photographers spent three years on the documentary in Alberta, a temperate and landlocked province of Canada.

After Eskimo children told the photographers the urban myth that lemmings undertake dramatic migrations culminating in mass suicide leaps off cliffs at the edge of the sea, the photographers decided that the compelling story, true or not, had to be told. They imported lemmings, small rodents not native to Alberta, placed them on snow-covered turntables and filmed them from various angles to create a sequence depicting migration. For the most famous sequence of the film, the photographers herded the lemmings over a cliff into a river cropped to look like the ocean while the narrator announced: "A kind of compulsion seizes each tiny rodent and, carried along by an unreasoning hysteria, each falls into step for a march that will take them to a strange destiny. ... They've become victims of an obsession—a one-track thought: Move on! Move on!"

By providing a script for life in extreme environments, such films make the banality and misery of nature entertaining and amusing. They tame the unimaginable sameness of the most inhospitable parts of the Earth, forming it into easily comprehensible stories for distant audiences in comfortable theaters and warm homes. This process continues today. In 2005, *March of the Penguins* became a worldwide hit by depicting the lives of pairs of emperor penguins as a love story. Although in the American release actor Morgan Freeman narrates the story of the penguins, in the original French version, director Luc Jacquet represented the emotions of the pairs through voice-overs by male and female actors. This film, too, has been criticized by scientists for its rampant anthropomorphism. Its detractors argue that many of the most moving moments, such as when the penguins appear to grieve over a broken egg or a doomed chick, are merely Terry Schiavo-like instinctive reactions that appear cute but demonstrate no real sign of emotion or understanding.

To be sure, these are only limit conditions, useful to us for unveiling the process by which "true-life" stories are told. But documentaries not only permeate television channels, their strategies infiltrate our lives. The rise of our fascination with non-fiction is accompanied by our dawning awareness that reality is itself scripted, created according to the conventions of fictions. As in *Nanook of the North*, *White Wilderness*, or *March of the Penguins*, fiction does not so much disappear as it is sublated into reality.

Our contemporary fascination with the documentary does not mean that we take the world as it is, but rather reminds us that what appears to be reality itself is invented. Slavoj Žižek has written, "...it is not only that Hollywood stages a semblance of real life deprived of the weight and inertia of materiality—in the late capitalist consumerist society, 'real social life' itself somehow acquires the features of a staged fake, with our neighbors behaving in 'real' life as stage actors and extras... [T]he ultimate truth of the capitalist utilitarian de-spiritualized universe is the de-materialization of the 'real life' itself, its reversal into a spectral show."[1] In our hyper-saturated media environment, the real is constructed by media, and anything constructed by media is made real.

Believing that reality is scripted gives us bounds. If there is an order to things on reality TV, then it must be so in our lives. If there is an underlying

[1] Slavoj Žižek, *Welcome to the Desert of the Real* (New York: Verso, 2002), 13-14.

author, we are relieved of the responsibility of having to make all of our own decisions. If reality can be edited, no action is irrevocable. We take comfort in knowing that we share in the same problems as others and that problems like our own are worthy of media coverage. Everyone's lives become equal to everyone else's. Like the novel or the documentary, in order to tell a compelling story and to make our world comprehensible, we preplan, script, and edit our lives, thereby making a compelling story out of the drudgery of everyday life. After reading an article about trouble in relationships, we throw a wrench into our own. The resulting problem has to be worked out, thereby relieving monotony while making us feel like a part of something greater. Perhaps, documentaries even suggest, our lives might be of sufficient interest to be capitalized, sold to the highest bidder as the basis for smash Hollywood hits.

In order to keep going in a world where every desire and every decision is valid, we have to creatively bring a sense of order to our lives. Non-fiction allows us to believe that the stories we tell ourselves about our existence have meaning and importance. The stories of the brave Nanook, the determined lemmings, and the loving penguins are models to aspire too, offering hope that like filmmakers in the polar regions, we too can make sense out of the banality of everyday life.

INTRODUCTION

AUDC formed in January 2001 as an informal research unit at the Southern California Institute of Architecture where Robert Sumrell was a graduate student and Kazys Varnelis was teaching and running the Program in History and Theory of Architecture and Cities. In the polar wilderness of contemporary life, like lemmings, we were driven by a single compulsion, to understand the predicament of the individual through architecture. We found our time working together, in studio as well as in courses we taught, immensely productive and—with Robert's graduation upon us—created AUDC to continue our collaboration. These were the last, heady days of the Clinton administration—it was hard to imagine that Bush could conceivably do any harm— a delirious period of optimism, perhaps the last time that America will ever be that optimistic again.

Our naïve first thought was that we would compete with Rem Koolhaas's AMO, operating as a consultancy or design practice. We called ourselves Architecture Urbanism Design Collaborative (AUDC), a name we intended to have as few connotations as possible.[1] In doing this, we sought to use AUDC as an "ideological tool to enter territories where architecture has never entered" to appropriate Koolhaas's own description of AMO.[2] Like AMO, we were encouraged by the limitless bounds achieved by the dot-com industry. Surely we could do as well. But the handwriting was on the wall: Pets.com had already collapsed, NASDAQ was on its way down from its all-time high,

[1] To come clean about our name, we should explain that we spent an inordinate amount of time looking at names of rock bands. We decided that the most perfect name was AC/DC, but since that was already taken, we merely turned the second letter 90 degrees counterclockwise and removed the decorative slash. This was our first and last formal move.

[2] See Samira Chandwani, "Koolhaas Speaks on Global Style," *The Cornell Daily Sun*, April 26, 2005, http://www.cornellsun.com/vnews/display.v/ART/2005/04/26/426ddebcc1992

and AMO's web site for Prada remained shuttered. Within months, the dot-com bubble burst. A half-year later, the 9/11 attacks laid low our remaining optimism about the possibility of such a consultancy.

So what to do? We quickly dropped the get-rich-quick scheme of emulating AMO. We kept little from that post-critical time, save for the idea that meaningless acronyms were best. Given that architecture today is generally thought of as incapable of representation, we felt it appropriate that our name should also reflect this condition and communicate nothing. Hence, today AUDC means only AUDC.

Being an archaic remnant of the craft era, architecture is by necessity slow. So even as the dot-com boom imploded, architecture wound up infected by its worst impulses. Buoyed by profligate economic policies intended to prop up the teetering global economy, the most affluent generation in history, the Boomers (in Europe, the 68'ers), turned its mighty investment power from stocks to buildings, thereby feeding a frenzy of construction that would be greatly accelerated by insane lending policies such as the five year interest-only adjustable rate mortgage. Leveraged beyond belief, architecture itself became less and less real until it finally became as speculative as an investment in dog sock puppets during late 2000. For a generation of architects, this means that the crucial gestational period as they develop their practices is now a last-ditch rush toward whatever they can pass off as "new": new materials, new forms, new practices, new eyeglasses, new shoes. "Make it new" has become a mantra again, some seventy years after Ezra Pound first put the idea to paper, only this generation forgets that Pound ever said it and seems compulsively unable to make anything new.

Having learned our lesson once with the dot-com era and, watching in amazement as architecture increasingly became irreal, we could only seek ways out and turned to mapping our condition. We devised a practice that would not produce buildings—after all, who needs any more of them?—

but rather would undertake speculative research to reveal the contemporary condition. To be sure, AUDC never set out to make buildings. Even in our brief guise as a consultancy, our mission statement was and remains to this day, "AUDC constructs realities not objects." But neither did we intend to replicate the solipsistic "critical architecture" of the 1980s and 1990s, those empty squiggles accompanied by even more empty words. For in our eyes, the biggest legacy of critical architecture was to pave the way for the leveraging of architecture today. It is no accident that the architects associated with that time are now among our most successful.[3] For as Jean Baudrillard has taught us, the fragmentation of the sign is one with the logic of contemporary capital. Freeing buildings of their use value and of any pretense to meaning—a task deconstructivism began and supermodernism completed—allows them to float freely, existing in the realm of exchange value only, an ideal pretext for a building boom based on little more than fantasy.[4] After all, only when meaning and responsibility had been thoroughly evacuated from architecture could Daniel Libeskind seriously propose a 1,776 foot tall replacement for the World Trade Center towers.

Instead, then, we set out to use the tools of architecture and research to pry open entryways into new territories. More than anything, we thought, we could build on the unique ways of thinking inherent in architecture as a form of speculative research. For models, we turned to the *architettura radicale* of Archizoom and Superstudio. These groups intervened at a moment structurally parallel to our own. Just as our time comes at the end of post-Fordism and at the dawn of a new period of economic crisis, environmental

[3] Anthony Vidler observes the late boom in deconstructivist architecture in "Deconstruction Boom: Anthony Vidler On Deconstructivist Architecture In 2003," *ArtForum*, December 2003, 33.

[4] Jean Baudrillard, *For A Critique of the Political Economy of the Sign* (St. Louis: Telos Press, 1981), 156. See also Hal Foster, *Recodings* (Seattle: Bay Press, 1985), 6. On supermodernism, see Hans Ibelings, *Supermodernism* (Rotterdam: NAi Publishers, 1998).

collapse, and global antagonism to the United States, the late 1960s were the last years of Fordism, with the Vietnam war still a thorn—not yet a spear—in the US's side and the OPEC energy crisis still to come. Then, like today, many of the leading practitioners in architecture and design were fatally enthralled by the possibility of form as a generator of affect, of being able to appeal to a broader public by wearing the mantle of hip consumerism.[5]

Architettura radicale stood against this position while offering a way of practicing that went beyond either "going with the flow" or adopting the empty postures of academics. Instead, *architettura radicale* was founded on the principle of superarchitecture, "the architecture of superproduction, of superconsumption, of superinducement to consumption, of the super-market, of Superman, of super-high-test gasoline." In the words of Andrea Branzi, the founder of Archizoom, "Superarchitecture accepts the logic of production and consumption and makes an effort to demystify it." This integration of production and consumption into a critique of the same system, the pursuit not of resistance or autonomy but rather of exacerbation and overload was *architettura radicale's* seminal innovation, deployed repeatedly in subsequent projects such as the Continuous Monument or No-Stop-City. For Archizoom and Superstudio architecture is an act of analysis, not merely a project of formal delirium or self-legitimating theory.[6]

This was a time of immense opportunity for the 68ers, but it was also a period of closure for architecture. Fatally associated with Fordist big business and big government, modernism accompanied them in their collapse. Coupled with this, leftist critiques of planning and technology, most notably Manfredo Tafuri's pronouncement that architecture was dead, took

[5] Andrea Branzi, *The Hot House* (Cambridge, MA: The MIT Press, 1984), 49-55. On hip consumerism, see Thomas Frank, *The Conquest of Cool. Business Culture, Counterculture, and the Rise of Hip Consumerism* (Chicago: University of Chicago Press, 1997).

[6] Quoted in Branzi, *The Hot House*, 54.

the wind out of the sails of new practices. Branzi understood this moment, however not as punctual and final, but as a time of renewal. In a later interview, he recalls: "all the most vital aspects of modern culture run directly toward that void, to regenerate themselves in another dimension, to free themselves of their disciplinary chains. When I look at a canvas by Mark Rothko, I see a picture dissolving into a single color. When I read Joyce's *Ulysses*, I see writing disappearing into thought. When I listen to John Cage, I hear music dissipating into noise. All that is part of me. But architecture has never confronted the theme of managing its own death while still remaining alive, as all the other twentieth-century disciplines have. This is why it has lagged behind..." Like Archizoom, AUDC's investigations have always been at this vital periphery of architecture, at the moments when, exacerbated to breaking point, it may cease to be.[7]

During a time of "post-criticism," and "going with the flow," this flirtation with architecture's annihilation may seem thoroughly unacceptable. But as Freud points out, the drive of each organism is towards stillness and ultimately death. As organisms come to being from a plenum of inanimate matter, he hypothesizes, they possess a drive to return to this undifferentiated state, the death drive or pleasure principle. If, however, the organism experiences "the influx of fresh amounts of stimulus" through a traumatic moment such as a union with another, it can be irritated enough to go on living or, if the stimulus is strong enough, reproduce. In architecture's morbid fear of reflection and criticism and in its over-identification with a post-Fordist culture now nearing collapse under threat from a new networked society, we sense a moment as dangerous—and as pregnant—for architecture as that of the late 1960s and early 1970s. In this spirit,

[7] Andrea Branzi interviewed in François Burkhardt and Cristina Morozzi, *Andrea Branzi* (Paris: Éditions Dis Voir, 1997), 49-50. For a sustained analysis of Archizoom, see also Kazys Varnelis, "Programming after Program. Archizoom's No Stop City," *Praxis* 8, Spring 2006, 82-90.

then, we give this project as a gift to architecture, a challenge and a stimulus to a field that urgently needs to refresh itself.[8]

This is not to say that we do not find influences in our own time. On the contrary, we draw great inspiration from the work of young groups like Anarchitektur in Berlin, Valdas Ožarinskas and Aida Çeponyte in Vilnius, or Lewis Tsurumaki Lewis and Baxi / Martin in New York as well as by two Los Angeles institutions: the Museum of Jurassic Technology and the Center for Land Use Interpretation. Together, these collectives demonstrated to us the continued value of working collaboratively and the possibilities for speculative forms of research. In particular, the latter two institutions made it possible for us to think of the territory previously called art as fertile ground, recently emptied by a diet of bankrupt formalism and specious pseudo-critique (would you prefer a dissected shark in formaldehyde or a crucifix in a vat of urine today, sir?).

On the surface, both the Museum of Jurassic Technology and the Center for Land Use Interpretation could be considered art practices. They receive funding from sources traditionally associated with giving to the arts such as the LEF Foundation, the Andy Warhol Foundation for the Visual Arts, and the Lannan Foundation. Individuals working at these institutions often, although not always, have been educated in the arts such as photography or cinema. Art critics frequently praise the work of both and museum curators have included the Museum and the Center in shows. And yet, neither organization claims status as an art practice. Instead, both are organized around curatorial practices. The Museum is a cabinet-of-curiosities-like collection, a compilation that, according to its mission statement is "a specialized

---

[8] Sigmund Freud, *Beyond the Pleasure Principle*, trans. James Strachey, (New York: Liveright Pub. Corp., 1961), 52. For a lengthier discussion of the pleasure principle, especially with regard to Giorgio Agamben's theories of form and content, see also Kazys Varnelis, "Prada and the Pleasure Principle," *Log* 6, September 2005.

repository of relics and artifacts from the Lower Jurassic, with an emphasis on those that demonstrate unusual or curious technological qualities." These range from a show of artworks executed on the head of pins to an exhibit on a bat that can fly through lead by vibrating from the extreme ultraviolet into the x-ray range to a collection of collections from Los Angeles mobile home parks. Throughout, a nagging uncertainty about what is real and what is fake haunts the visitor. For its part, according to its mission statement, the Center for Land Use Interpretation is devoted to "exploring, examining, and understanding land and landscape issues. The Center employs a variety of methods to pursue its mission—engaging in research, classification, extrapolation, and exhibition." Recent exhibits have explored the remains of submerged towns in America, live footage of livestock, and soil in the margins of Los Angeles.[9]

Curation reflects a dominant condition of network culture: as the processes of globalization, urbanization (and dis-urbanization) and the hegemonization of the world under late capital have closed the last frontiers and, consequently, the new is played out, novelty is now created through aggregation and commentary. Digital technology aids greatly in this, making remixing part of everyday life for many individuals. Lev Manovich observes that the "emergence of multiple and interlinked paths which encourage media objects to easily travel between Web sites, recording and display devices, hard

---

[9] In the interest of historical accuracy, we should note that Kazys Varnelis undertook a five year long research project for the Center for Land Use Interpretation on the Owens River Valley and our work on Ether took form first as an exhibit on One Wilshire by Varnelis at the Center in 2002. Moreover, Steve Rowell, who helped us on occasion as a friendly interloper, is one of the directors of CLUI. On the Museum of Jurassic Technology see *The Museum of Jurassic Technology* (Primi Decem Anni, Jubilee Catalogue) (West Covina, Ca: Trustees of the Society for the Diffusion of Useful Information, 2001) and Lawrence Wechsler, *Mr. Wilson's Cabinet Of Wonder: Pronged Ants, Horned Humans, Mice on Toast, and Other Marvels of Jurassic Technology* (New York: Pantheon, 1995). The Center's work is documented in Matt Coolidge and Sarah Simons, *Overlook: Exploring the Internal Fringes of America with the Center for Land Use Interpretation* (New York: Metropolis Books, 2006). For an analysis, see Sarah Kanouse, "Touring the Archive, Archiving the Tour: Image, Text, and Experience with the Center for Land Use Interpretation," *Art Journal* 64, no 2 (Summer 2005): 78-87.

drives, and people changes things. Remixability becomes practically a built-in feature of the digital networked media universe. In a nutshell, what may be more important than the introduction of a video iPod, a consumer HD camera, Flickr, or yet another exiting new device or service is how easy it is for media objects to travel between all these devices and services—which now all become just temporary stations in media's Brownian motion."[10]

Bit players in this culture of curation and aggregation, we assembled a group of peculiar and compelling conditions and turned to investigating them. To be sure, we could have simply documented these conditions, but we chose not to do that. Instead we draw the reader's attention to a recent statement by Bruno Latour: "'Things' are controversial assemblages of entangled issues, and not simply objects sitting apart from our political passions. The entanglements of things and politics engage activists, artists, politicians, and intellectuals. To assemble this parliament, rhetoric is not enough and nor is eloquence; it requires the use of all the technologies—especially information technology—and the possibility for the arts to re-present anew what are the common stakes."[11] In that spirit, we felt obliged to respond with all the tools available to us: drawings, models, photography, historical research, and new media. In doing so, we affirm the value of architecture as a way of knowing and a means of research. To be clear, it is not architecture's task to explain these conditions through interventions. We do not seek a return to a semiotics of building. Just as the set is essential to any film, however, it is possible to use architecture—models and drawings—as part of a process of speculative research.

So too, we have let the different sites for our work—articles, public installations and exhibits, lectures, videos and the Web impact the way we

[10] Lev Manovich, "Remix and Remixability," Rhizome-Rare Mailing List. http://rhizome.org/thread.rhiz?thread=19303&page=1

[11] Bruno Latour, http://rhizome.org/print/?36087.

work. Of these, the Web merits particular mention for it has not just been a site to deploy our work on, it has been a venue to work in. In 2004, we deployed wiki software on our site to allow us to work collaboratively on-line. Invented by Ward Cunningham in 1995, a WikiWikiWeb, or Wiki, is a communal, hypertext repository of knowledge on the Web. "Wiki wiki" means fast in Hawaiian. Employing a simplified subset of HTML and markup within the Web browser itself, a wiki page is much faster to develop than most Web pages. Moreover, wikis are editable by multiple individuals and generally actively encourage anyone who visits them to contribute. Cunningham's project, the Portland Pattern Repository, inspired by architect Christopher Alexander's idea of a pattern language for designing buildings and cities, gathered information on design patterns, recurring solutions to problems in object-oriented design programming. The most well-known wiki is Wikipedia. org, perhaps the largest collaborative work in human history, consisting of more than 3,380,000 articles, including more than 985,000 in the English-language version (as an example of network culture, it bears mentioning that Wikipedia editorial policy is firmly against any idea of creating new understanding or creating definitive positions, but instead clings firmly to the ideal of a "neutral point of view" for all articles). Using Mediawiki software, the same software that runs the Wikipedia, albeit heavily modified for our purposes with support from the Institute for Multimedia Literacy and the Annenberg Center for Communication, we wrote the bulk of these texts online. We initially hoped to open up the wiki so that others, even unknown others, could contribute, but even though we gave access to it to a number of individuals, we found that they didn't contribute (the sum total of three months of input was one period mark added to a sentence) and that unlike Wikipedia, our own project thrived on a distinct point-of-view that was emerging out of our collaboration. The virtue of the wiki as a collaborative tool remains, however, as it is a useful means of breaking down the idea of sole authorship, which is increasingly an artifact of the past. We are much more interested in the hybrid, subjectless process of writing that emerges through the wiki. More and more texts—virtually all scientific and engineering papers, as well as many of the great recent works in the humanities such as *A Thousand Plateaus* or *Empire*—are written by entities that are greater than the sum of their authors. Moreover, wikis inherently tend toward nonlinear navigational structures, something we took advantage of in creating a navigational structure for the site. But we also found that narratives are a time-tested method of telling stories that people naturally gravitate to. To this end, the last three months of writing took place on Writely.com, a Web-based word processor that allows real-time, networked collaboration on more traditional documents.

As we looked at the various conditions we encountered, we realized that they were illustrative of broader themes in contemporary culture: a dissipation of the subject, the proliferation of object culture, the rise of the digital, the Dadaist nature of the contemporary economy, and the fictionalization of the world. But as Keller Easterling points out, this is dangerous territory. Architecture has a fatal attraction to monist explanations. The master narratives of Deleuze and Guattari's *Thousand Plateaus* and Hardt and Negri's *Empire* are as appealing to architects as the relentless geometry of screen-based animation programs. Builders by nature, architects tend to weave theories together into improbable grand narratives. As in the autonomy theory of the early 1970s, theory, in this guise, is generally a means of self-legitimation, an elaborate affirmation of whatever form is being extruded that day.[12]

Easterling's warning is needed, but then how to negotiate the territory of contemporary philosophy? We are certainly attracted to Deleuze and Guattari's organizational logics and Hardt and Negri's tales of Empire as well

12 Keller Easterling, *Enduring Innocence. Global Architecture and its Political Masquerades* (Cambridge, MA: The MIT Press, 2005), 8-10.

as to Baudrillard's theories of totalized consumption of the sign and the system of objects, Žižek's fictionalization of the real, and Jameson's dissection of late capitalism. These are fascinating explanatory frameworks, but, scandalously, they don't add up. To weave a coherent whole out of them would be sheer madness. So how to proceed?

During our research into the evolution of art, science, and philosophy we found that these fields were once much more intimately related than they had been in the last century. Prior to the Enlightenment and the development of the scientific method, science was dominated by natural philosophy, a method of studying nature and the physical universe through observation rather than through experimentation. Virtually all contemporary forms of science developed out of natural philosophy, but unlike more modern scientists, natural philosophers like Galileo felt no need to test their ideas in a practical way. On the contrary, they derived philosophical conclusions from individual observations of the world. Taken together, these didn't necessarily add up. But the lack of metanarrative for natural philosophy is not an obstacle for us, instead it is a strength, encouraging further investigation instead of satiating desire.

Natural philosophy flourished from the twelfth to the seventeenth centuries and with it did "cabinets of curiosities," sometimes entire rooms, sometimes quite literally elaborate cabinets, filled with strange and wondrous things. These first museums collected seemingly disparate objects of fascination in a specific architectural setting, assigning to each item a place in a larger network of meaning created by the room as a whole. In the cabinet, each object would be a macrocosm of the larger world, illustrating the wonder of its divine artifice. Together however, their affinities would become apparent and a syncretic vision of the unity of all things would emerge, as the words Athanasius Kircher inscribed on the ceiling of his museum suggested: "Whosoever perceives the chain that binds the world below to the world above will know the mysteries of nature and achieve miracles." For the natural philosopher, the cabinet of curiosities possessed a reflexive quality: it was both an exhibition and a source of wonder, a system the natural philosopher built to instruct others but also to coax himself into further thought.[13]

Like our Web site (http://www.audc.org) or an AUDC installation, this book is a cabinet of curiosities, consisting of a series of conditions that AUDC observes in order to speculate on them in the manner of natural philosophy, extrapolating not theories to apply to architecture but rather philosophies to explain the world. The result is neither relativist pluralism nor a single monist philosophy, but rather a set of multiple philosophies that almost add up, but being situationally derived, don't quite.

What follows then, is a book of non-fiction fables, collecting three stories—Ether, the Stimulus Progression, and Swarm Intelligence—that touch on our daily lives along with three brief interludes—My Dear Berlin Wall, Voluntary Slavery, and Mike—to illustrate the ways that people relate to each other and to the world around them. The three interludes are hopeless causes, each a story of damaged love for an object: a Swedish woman's marriage to the Berlin Wall, a collector's obsessive desire for his records, and a farmer's devotion to a headless chicken. The three longer stories explore One Wilshire, the place where the Internet becomes physical while we become media; Muzak, the soundtrack to daily life as well as an invisible reshaper of cities; and Quartzsite, Arizona, an instant city based on the exchange of rocks. These three are intimately connected to architecture yet remain outside of it—a banal office building, a kitschy soundtrack, a brutally anti-aesthetic patch of desert filled with motorhomes. Architecture is unnecessary

---

[13] Patrick Mauries, *Cabinets of Curiosities* (New York: Thames and Hudson, 2002), 25-26. Some further sources on cabinets of curiosities are Lorraine Daston and Katherine Park, *Wonders and the Order of Nature* (Cambridge: The MIT Press, 1998) and Giorgio Agamben, "The Cabinet of Wonder" in *The Man Without Content* (Stanford: Stanford University Press, 1999), 28-39.

to them and to make standard architectural responses in them would be absurd. But that is precisely what draws us these stories—each one is a self-sufficient utopia that threatens to take over the world. Using research and speculation, we seek the organizational logics that motivate them, as well as the disorganizational factors that doom them. Their total conditions—the virtual world of the Internet, the all-pervasive nature of Muzak, and the threat of ephemerality and arbitrariness that Quartzsite levels at the contemporary city—exemplify the outcroppings of Empire that remain hidden in plain sight. Although—with the exception of the interlude on the Berlin Wall—these conditions are found in the United States, we claim no priority for that save for Antonio Negri and Michael Hardt's suggestion that if Empire had a dominant country, it would be the United States.[14] There is nothing particularly American about our stories; to the contrary, they all have global implications. But we don't set out to justify our parochialism, rather we beg the reader to excuse us. We found most of the objects of study in *Blue Monday* near Los Angeles, our first base. Now that AUDC has moved to the Northeastern seaboard and spawned the AUDC Network Architecture Laboratory at Columbia University's Graduate School of Architecture, Preservation, and Planning, our focus will shift accordingly. This book, then, marks the completion of the first phase of AUDC's work.

In the end, our hope for this book is that it will arouse in our readers the same sense of wonder and amazement that has compelled us on our own lemming-like quest to investigate these subjects, thereby encouraging them to consider further the world of Empire.

[14] Antonio Hardt and Michael Negri, *Empire* (Cambridge, MA: Harvard University Press, 2000), xiii-xiv .

ABSTRACTION

<>

MY DEAR BERLIN WALL

ETHER:
One Wilshire

MY DEAR BERLIN WALL

On June 17, 1979, Eija-Riita Eklöf, a Swedish woman, married the Berlin Wall
at Groß-Ziethener Straße, taking Wall Winther Berliner-Mauer as her name.
The final piece of heroic modernist architecture, the Berlin Wall was construct-
ed just as the movement's Utopian political ambitions had begun to wane.
By then, with the eastward spread of modernism during the Khrushchev years,
the ideological distinctiveness of modernity had come to an end, making East-
West, modern–antimodern harder to distinguish. Still, the architects of the
Berlin Wall hoped it would change society.

For a while, it did just that. After the close of World War II, Berlin was a
microcosm of Germany. Both city and country were cut into four occupation
zones, each overseen by a commander-in-chief from one of the four Allied powers, the United States, the United Kingdom, France, and the Union of Soviet
Socialist Republics. As the geopolitical tide continued to shift in the years
after the war, tensions escalated between the Soviets and the Western allies.
By the time of the Berlin Blockade of 1948-1949, it became clear that the three
allied segments of Berlin would become "West Berlin," an enclave of the Federal Republic of Germany (or "West Germany") while the Soviet-controlled sector
would become "East Berlin," associated with the German Democratic
Republic (or "East Germany"). Responding to the blockade crisis, Belgium,
Canada, Denmark, France, Iceland, Italy, Luxembourg, Netherlands, Norway,
Portugal, United Kingdom, and the United States promised mutual military

defense through the North Atlantic Treaty Organization (NATO) in 1949.

In 1955, West Germany joined NATO and, in response, the Soviet Union formed the Warsaw Pact with Albania, Bulgaria, Czechoslovakia, Hungary, Poland, and Romania. East Germany joined one year later as two events cemented the division of the world. The first was the Suez Crisis in which the United States, fearing thermonuclear war with the Soviet Union, forced France and Britain to withdraw from the Suez Canal, a critical piece of infrastructure they had occupied earlier that year to prevent Egypt from nationalizing it. The second was the Hungarian Revolution, crushed by Soviet tanks as the West watched. With the refusal of the Soviet Union and the United States to enter into direct confrontation, it became clear that the world, Europe, Germany, and Berlin had been divided into spheres of influence controlled by the superpowers.

The superpowers fought the Cold War through their display of achievements in science, propaganda, and accumulation. Berlin became the prime place for the two competing rivals to showcase their material culture. In the East, the Stalinallée, designed by architects Hartmann, Henselmann, Hopp, Leucht, Paulick and Souradny, was a nearly 2 km-long 89 m-wide boulevard lined with eight-story Socialist Classicist buildings. Inside these vast structures, workers enjoyed luxurious apartments, shops, and restaurants. In response, West Berlin held the Interbau exhibit in 1957, assembling the masters of modern architecture including Alvar Aalto, Walter Gropius, Le Corbusier, Oscar Niemeyer, Johannes van den Broek and Jaap Bakema, Egon Eiermann, and Pierre Vago to build a model modernist community of housing blocks in a park in the Hansaviertel quarter.

Nor was the battle of lifestyle between East and West limited to architecture. Soviet communism followed capitalism to focus on industrial productivity and expansion within a newly global market. While the United States exported its products—and eventually outsourced its production—throughout the world, the Soviets used COMECON, the economic equivalent of the Warsaw Pact, to eliminate trade barriers among communist countries. Each country produced objects to represent its superior quality of life, validating each system not only to its own citizens, but also to each other and to the rest of the world. The importance of material culture in the Cold War is underscored by the 1959 Nixon-Khrushchev "Kitchen Debate," played out between the two powers in a demonstration kitchen at a model house during the American National Exhibit in Moscow. At the impromptu debate, Soviet Premier Nikita Khrushchev expressed his disgust by the heavily automated kitchen and asked if there was a machine that "puts food into the mouth and pushes it down." U. S. Vice President Richard Nixon responded, "Would it not be better to compete in the relative merits of washing machines than in the strength of rockets?" A Cold War battle was fought through house wares.[1]

The climax of the battle came in Berlin. In the divided city, half a million people would go back and forth each day between East and West. Westerners would shop in East Berlin where products, subsidized by the East Bloc, were cheap. Easterners would shop in the Western sector where fetish items such as

[1] Elaine Tyler May, *Homeward Bound: American Families in the Cold War Era* (New York: Basic Books, 1999), 10-12.

seamless nylons and tropical fruits could be found. Overall, however, the flow was westward. The rate of defection was unstoppable: between 1949 and 1961 some 2.5 million East Germaners left for the West, primarily through Berlin. But just as destructive was the mass flight of subsidized objects westward, a migration that pushed the inefficient communist system to collapse. Khrushchev had won the debate: cheap goods from the East were more desirable, but the cost to the system was unacceptable. By this time, production and accumulation in the East Bloc had became goals in and of themselves, devoid of logic and use, no longer tied to the basic needs of the economy. In 1961, Khrushchev launched the Third Economic Program to increase the Soviet Union's production of industrial goods at all costs. During a meeting that year, COMECON decided that the flow of people and products had to be stopped. On August 13, 1961 the border was sealed with a barrier constructed by East German troops.

The result was a city divided in two without regard for prior form or use. Over time, the Berlin Wall evolved from barbed wire fences (1961-1965) to a concrete wall (1965-1975), until it reached its full maturity in 1975. The final form would be not one but two Walls, each constructed from 45,000 3.6 meter high by 1.5 meter wide sections of reinforced concrete, each weighing 2.75 tons, separated by a no-man's-land as wide as 91 meters. The Wall was capped by a smooth pipe, making it difficult to scale and was accompanied by fences, trenches and barbed wire as well as over 300 watchtowers and thirty bunkers.[2]

Thomas Flemming, *The Berlin Wall: Division of a City* (Berlin: be.bra Verlag, 2000), 75

With its utopian aspiration to change society, the Wall was the last product of heroic modernism. It succeeded in changing society, but as with most modernist products, not in the way its builders intended. East Berlin, open to the larger body of the East Bloc, withered, becoming little more than a vacation wonderland for the Politburo élite of the Soviet Union and Warsaw Pact and a playground for spies of both camps. Cut off, West Berlin thrived. By providing a datum line for Berlin, the Wall gave meaning to the lives of its inhabitants. In recognition of this, Joseph Beuys proposed that the Wall should be made taller by 5 cm for "aesthetic purposes." [3]

As the Wall was being constructed in Berlin, Situationists in Paris and elsewhere were advocating for radical changes in cities as a means of preserving urban life. For them, the aesthetics of modernism and the forces of modernity were destroying urbanity itself. During this period working-class Paris was being emptied out, its inhabitants sent by the government to an artificial modernist city in the suburbs while an equally artificial cultural capital for tourists and industry was created in the cleaned-up center. Led by Guy Debord, the Situationists hoped to recapture the city by creating varied ambiances and environments together with strategies providing opportunities for stimulation and chance drift. When Situationist architect Constant Nieuwenhuys deployed the floating transparent layers of his New Babylon to augment the existing city with unique, flexible, and transient spaces, Debord condemned the project, ar-

---

[3] Irving Sandler, *Art of the Postmodern Era* (Boulder, CO: Westview Press, 1998), 110.

guing that the existing city was already almost perfect. Only minor modifica-
tions, were necessary, such as adding light switches to street lights so that they
could be turned on and off at will and allowing people to wander in subways
after they were shut off at night.

In his 1972 thesis at the Architectural Association, entitled "Exodus, or the
Voluntary Prisoners of Architecture," Rem Koolhaas found a way of reconciling
modernism with Situationism through the figure of the Wall. Suggesting that
the Wall might be exported to London and made to encircle it, Koolhaas writes,
"The inhabitants of this architecture, those strong enough to love it, would become its Voluntary Prisoners, ecstatic in the freedom of their architectural con-
fines." Inside, life would be "a continuous state of ornamental frenzy and decorative delirium, an overdose of symbols." Although officially proposing a way
of making London more interesting, Koolhaas's thesis is really a set of observations about the already existing condition of the real Wall. [4]

In choosing to encircle London with the Wall, Koolhaas recognized that
it was not only the last great product of modernism, it was the last work of
heavy architecture. Already in 1966, in his introduction to *40 Under 40*, Robert Stern observed that an increasingly dematerialized "cardboard architecture" was "the order of the day" in the United States while in England, architects such as Archigram were proposing barrier-less technological utopias. [5]

[4] Rem Koolhaas, *S, M, L, XL* (New York: Monacelli, 1995), 2-21.

[5] Robert A.M. Stern, ed., *40 Under 40: An Exhibition of Young Talent in Architecture*
(New York: The Architectural League of New York, 1966), VII.

Built of concrete, the wall was solid, weighty. It hearkened back to the days of the medieval city walls, which were not only defensive but attempted to organize and contain a world progressively more interconnected through communications and trade. Walls acted as concentrators, defining places in which early capitalism and urbanity could be found and intensifying both. So long as the modes of communication remained physical and the methods of making and trading goods were slow, nations retained their authority and autonomy through architectural solidity.

The destruction of the Berlin Wall in 1989 is concurrent with the pervasive and irreversible spread of Empire and the end of heavy architecture. Effectively, the Wall fell by accident. During 1989, mass demonstrations in East Germany led to the resignation of East German leader Erich Honecker. Soon, border restrictions between neighboring nations were lifted and the new government decided to allow East Berliners to apply for visas to visit West Germany. On November 9, 1989, East German Minister of Propaganda Günter Schabowski accidentally unleashed the Wall's destruction. Shortly before a televised press conference, the Minister was handed a note outlining new travel regulations between East and West Berlin. Having recently returned from vacation, Schabowski did not have a good grasp on the enormity of the demonstrations in East Berlin or on the policy being outlined in the note. He decided to read the note aloud at the end of his speech, including a section stating that free travel would be allowed across the border. Not knowing how to properly answer questions as to when these new regulations would come into effect, he simply responded, "As far as I know effective immediately, right now." Tens of thousands of people crowded the checkpoints at the Wall and demanded entry, overwhelming border guards. Unwilling to massacre the crowds, the guards yielded, ending the Wall's power.[6]

Schabowski's mistake points to the underlying reason for the Wall's collapse: the lack of information flow in the East Bloc. The goals of Khrushchev's Third Economic Program were finally met by the early 1980s, but by that point the United States was no longer interested in production. For America, the manufacturing of objects proved to be more lucrative when outsourced to the developing world. By sending its production overseas, America assured the success of its ideology in the global sphere while concentrating on the production of the virtual. Having spent itself on production of objects, as well as on more bluntly applied foreign aid, the Soviet Union collapsed. Manuel Castells observes that, "in the 1980s the Soviet Union produced substantially more than the U. S. in a number of heavy industrial sectors: it produced 80 percent more steel, 78 percent more cement, 42 percent more oil, 55 percent more fertilizer, twice as much pig iron, and five times as many tractors." The problem, he concludes, was that material culture no longer mattered. The PC revolution was completely counter to the Soviet Union's centralization while photocopy machines were in the hands of the KGB.[7]

[6] Angela Stent, *Russia and Germany Reborn: Unification, the Soviet Collapse, and the New Europe* (Princeton: Princeton University Press, 1999), 94-96.

[7] Manuel Castells, *End of Millennium*, Second Edition (Oxford, UK: Blackwell, 2000), 26-27, See also the entire chapter on "The Crisis of Industrial Statism and the Collapse of the Soviet Union," 5-67.

With the Wall gone, and with it the division between East and West undone, the world is permeated by flows of information. Physical borders no longer hold back the flow of an immaterial capital. Indeed, soon after the Wall fell, the European Union set about in earnest to do away with borders between individual nation states.

But through it all, the Wall has had no greater fan than Wall Winther Berliner-Mauer. In her view, the Wall allowed peace to be maintained between East and West. As soldiers looked over the Wall to the other side, they saw men just like themselves, with families they loved and wanted to protect. In this way, the Wall created a bond between men who would otherwise be faceless enemies. But Berliner-Mauer's love for the Wall is far from abstract. For her, objects aren't inert but rather can possess souls and become individuals to fall in love with. Berliner-Mauer sees the Wall as a noble being and says she is erotically attracted to his horizontal lines and sheer presence. While Berliner-Mauer is in a seemingly extreme, sexual relationship with the object of her desire, our animistic belief in objects is widespread across society. Adults and children alike confide in stuffed animals, yell at traffic signs, and stroke their sports cars all the time. Many people choose to love objects over their friends, their spouses, or themselves. Berliner-Mauer understands that the role of objects in our lives has changed. Objects are no longer tools that stand in to do work for us, or surrogates for normal human activities. Objects have come into their own, and as such we have formed new kinds of relationships with them that do not have a precedent in human interaction. The Wall is a loving presence in her life, and she loves it in return.

Faced with the tragedy of the Wall's destruction, Berliner-Mauer created a technique she calls "Temporal Displacement" to fix her mind permanently in the period during which the Wall existed, even at the cost of creating new memories.[8] For Berliner-Mauer, marrying the Wall is a last means to preserve the clarity of modernism and the effectiveness of architecture as a solid and heavy means of organization. To love the Berlin Wall is to dream of holding onto the simple, clear disciplinary regime of order and punishment that came before we were all complicit within the system. In today's society of control, as Gilles Deleuze writes, we don't need enclosures any more. Instead, we live in a world of endless modulations, internalizing control in order to direct ourselves instead of being directed.[9] After the fall of the Wall and the end of enclosures, even evil itself, Jean Baudrillard observes, loses its identity and spreads evenly through culture. An Other space is gone from the world. North Korea and Cuba are mere leftovers, relegated to tourism. There is nowhere to defect to: without the Wall, we must all face our own complicity in the system.[10]

---

[8] http://www.berlinermauer.se

[9] Gilles Deleuze, "Postscript on the Societies of Control," *October* 59 (Winter 1992), 3-7.

[10] Jean Baudrillard, "The Thawing of the East," *The Illusion of the End* (Stanford: Stanford University Press, 1994), 28-33.

ETHER: One Wilshire

If the Berlin Wall symbolized the division of the world by the superpowers during the Cold War, the Bomb guaranteed that division. By promising massive nuclear retaliation if the Soviet Union were to invade Europe, the United States ensured that the continent and world remained divided.

Beyond its brute firepower, the Bomb possessed the singular ability to erase an enemy. While burning had been a common means of disposing of humans since prehistory, vaporizing them so that nothing would be left behind was unprecedented. At Hiroshima, for the first time, people were transformed into pure energy, leaving behind only an occasional shadow recording the force of the blast. After the Bomb, matter's permanence would no longer be assured.

The Bomb spawned its own hysterical logic of accumulation and virtuality. Nuclear weapons became ever bigger and ever more numerous in order to assure not just destruction, but complete overkill. Overkill evolved into Mutually Assured Destruction (MAD), a guarantee that the surplus of nuclear exchange would thoroughly destroy both sides. By the 1970s, it was rumored that the Soviet Union had deployed a cobalt-salted bomb in East Berlin, a doomsday weapon whose location was purely symbolic as its intense radioactivity would have extinguished life on Earth if detonated. In contrast, American scientists developed the neutron bomb, an enhanced radiation device that would produce massive short-term radioactivity while minimizing blast damage and fallout, preserving more objects while killing more people.

The massive buildup of the Bomb, easily the most expensive undertaking in human history, was a proliferation of objects precisely at the time when they were becoming obsolete. In the virtual world, the Cold War became hot over and over again through software games in the computers both sides developed to wage simulations of nuclear battles. In the computer, the destructive potential of the warheads would be endlessly tested, adjusted, and retested. Militaries came to rely on the results of these tests as not just "scenario plans" but as victories and defeats themselves. In Orwellian fashion, however, defeat was victory: annihilation in the computer gave generals grounds to argue for further weapons development. Plausible truths regarding the strength of the enemy became more valuable than actual figures. Thus, both the "Bomber Gap" and the "Missile Gap" were convenient fictions, agreed upon by the Soviet and American military to make the former appear more threatening and to help the latter gain support for more weaponry. [1]

The Cold War ensured the shift from the material world to the virtual. Even though the Soviet Union outproduced it in the end, the United States won because it understood that the nature of production changed from physical objects to a virtual system of networks. If the dawn of the bourgeois era is marked by the development of the metropolis and the proliferation of objects, our own period begins with the emergence of the posturban realm and the economic dominance of immaterial production. Today the physical is secondary to systems of computation and communication.

Under threat of the Bomb, the concentrated, vertical city of congestion gave way to the dispersed, horizontal decongested field. During the Second World War, the Allied air offensive ground the Nazi war machine to a halt by hitting concentrated centers of production. Understanding that the United States was vulnerable to similar attack, after the first Soviet atomic bomb test in 1949 and the entry of the United States into the Korean War in 1950, defense analysts at the National Security Resources Board began to advocate the dispersal of new industries. By removing industry, and later management, from the city, planners hoped that target zones would be minimized. The nation, in their words, would be "protected in space." Urbanity as the product of concentrated structures and physical connections was replaced by an urbanity constituted through a system of dispersed virtual links.

[1] On the Cold War, see Martin Walker, *The Cold War. A History* (New York: Henry Holt and Company, 1994).

A NETWORKED SOCIETY

To facilitate this urban dispersal, President Dwight D. Eisenhower spear-headed the Federal-Aid Highway Act of 1956 to ensure the construction of the world's first transcontinental highway system. Eisenhower was alarmed by the congested nature of existing roads and felt that they were a hazard, with "appalling inadequacies to meet the demands of catastrophe or defense, should an atomic war come." After the Act, highway designers would studiously avoid city centers or other areas that could be targets of nuclear attack. [2] In proposing the Act to Congress, Eisenhower argued that it was America's destiny to be a networked society:

> Our unity as a nation is sustained by free communication of thought and by easy transportation of people and goods. The ceaseless flow of information throughout the republic is matched by individual and commercial movement over a vast system of interconnected highways crisscrossing the country and joining at our national borders with friendly neighbors to the north and south.
>
> Together, the united forces of our communication and transportation systems are dynamic elements in the very name we bear—United States. Without them, we would be a mere alliance of many separate parts. [3]

Calling for 41,000 miles of highway to be constructed across the United States in order to interconnect all of its major cities and industrial areas and to establish better links with strategic points in Canada and Mexico, the Act would be the largest building project ever undertaken and would assure the transformation of the United States to a dispersed posturban field.

[2] Peter Galison, "War Against the Center," *Grey Room* 04, Summer 2001, 6-33.

[3] Dwight D. Eisenhower, in Fred L. Israel and J. F. Watts, eds., *Presidential Documents: The Speeches, Proclamations and Policies That Have Shaped the Nation from Washington to Clinton* (New York: Routledge, 2000), 298-300.

Concentrated cores dominated not only the physical but also the telecommunicational realm. Dispersal of the latter would prove more difficult. From the start of the Bell system in the late nineteenth century, individual telephones have been connected to exchanges at a neighborhood "Company Office" (to this day, the distance from the Company Office determines the maximum speed of a DSL connection). In turn these exchanges link to a switching station in the city center, where the greatest concentration of phones can be found. Central switching stations in disparate cities would be linked by long distance lines that, beginning in the 1910s, were multiplexed, that is, able to transmit multiple simultaneous messages over a single cable—technology first developed by General George Owen Squier, then Chief Signal Officer of the Army's Signal Corps and the future founder of the Muzak Corporation.

After World War II, rising demand for bandwidth and a mounting fear of the havoc nuclear war would wreak on continuous wire connections led telecommunication engineers to develop microwave transmission for long distances. In 1947, the first microwave line was deployed between the headquarters of the American Telephone and Telegraph (AT&T) company's Long Lines Department at 32 Avenue of the Americas and the Bowdoin Square building of the New England Telephone and Telegraph through seven intermediately spaced relay stations. The experiment was a success and during the 1950s and early 1960s, AT&T moved to microwave towers for a large part of its

Long Lines network. Adopting the motto "Communications is the foundation of democracy," AT&T saw Long Lines as a crucial defense mechanism in the Cold War. Flagpoles adorned each installation, but this was not mere bluster. Long Lines installations were hardened against nuclear blasts with some even built underground. Microwave horns were covered with protective shields to prevent fallout from contaminating electronics within and shielded in copper against electromagnetic pulses targeted to disrupt electronic communications. In 1962, AT&T launched Telstar, the world's first commercial communications satellite, which they hoped would permit connections between any two points on the earth at any time and further increase communications survivability after atomic war. Ironically, Telstar would fail early due to radiation from Starfish Prime, a high altitude nuclear test conducted by the United States Army the day before Telstar's launch.

Soon after, Paul Baran, a researcher at the RAND corporation, a Cold War think tank, formulated a key plan to realize a networked model of communication that could survive nuclear attack. Baran feared that the highly centralized model of communications used by both civilian and military telephone systems was vulnerable. One good hit on a city center would ensure that communications would be destroyed.

In its place, Baran developed a system of distributed communications in which each point functions as a node, the network's common functions dispersed equally among the nodes. Designed not for present efficiency but for future survivability even after heavy damage during nuclear war, Baran's system breaks messages down into discrete units or "packets" and routes them on redundant paths to their destinations. With expected transmission errors a fact of life in a post-Apocalyptic environment, his system allow damaged portions of a message—instead of the whole thing—to be resent. Following the model of urban decentralization, nodes would be located in the countryside, avoiding vulnerable city centers. In everyday operation, Baran's "packet switching" system has the advantage of allowing individual sections of messages to be rerouted or even retransmitted when necessary and, as computers tend to communicate to each other in short bursts, takes advantage of slowdowns and gaps in communication to optimize the load on the lines.[4]

Baran's distributed network was meant to preserve hierarchy, not undo it. His goal was to maintain the centralized, top-down chain of command so that the other alternative—giving individual commanders in the field authority over nuclear weapons—would not be necessary. A victim of politics, Baran's network was never built as he envisioned it, but his basic idea of the distributed network and packet switching would be incorporated into ARPANET, the first successful inter-city data communications network.

Established after the launch of Sputnik to recapture U. S. scientific superiority, the Department of Defense's Advanced Research Projects Agency (DARPA) funded science and engineering programs in universities throughout the country, spurring on the development of high technology through projects such as the Orion nuclear powered rocket. To build community and overcome isolation between the fifteen offices of the Information Processing Techniques Office, the program funded ARPANET to link together researchers working with computers. ARPANET's planners hoped that community would emerge through the experience of working together informally with shared resources. Developed to make remote time-sharing of resources work more smoothly, email soon became the network's primary use.

Although ARPANET fostered a more distributed culture, encouraging informal, bottom-up management and interventions into the net, the model of distributed communications could not be fully implemented. ARPANET itself was distributed, but it was designed as an abstract layer, not as a separate physical network built from the ground up. Instead, it used exist-

[4] Paul Baran, "On Distributed Communications Networks," *IEEE Transactions on Communication Systems*, CS-12, 1964.

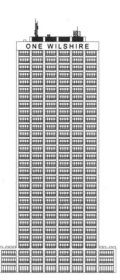

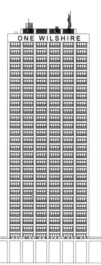

Abstraction – Ether: One Wilshire

ing long distance telephone lines leased from AT&T that, in accordance with the centralized model created a century earlier, joined switching stations in city cores. Had a nuclear war taken place, ARPANET would have been destroyed immediately.

Moreover, ARPANET emphasized the use of Interface Message Processors (IMPs), mini-computer interfaces allowing locally-based hosts to interface with the network. As there was generally only one IMP per city, the effect was that if ARPANET as a whole was distributed, at the local level it was highly centralized. Failure of an IMP not only meant that local hosts would fail to reach remote machines, it ensured they could not communicate with each other.

By the mid-1970s, research-oriented networks such as ARPANET and the National Science Foundation's NSFNet proliferated. Eventually these diverse networks would be linked by a single network of networks dubbed the Internet. NSFNet's rapid growth during the 1970s made it the dominant entity in

Abstraction – Ether: One Wilshire

the early Internet. The NSF implemented communications between regional networks through a "backbone" leased on lines from AT&T and offered central hubs in each city to which local users would connect. The result was the final undoing of the distributed model. [5]

With the privatization of the Internet in the 1990s, network topology has continued to centralize. Driven by profit, the need to build rapidly, and shackled by the difficulties of negotiations for new rights-of-way, telecommunications carriers follow existing systems of networking established by telephony. Interconnections are between major nodes located in city cores. Within cities, fiber optics can be laid down more inexpensively and higher capacity, short-distance networks can be built relatively easily. If, following AT&T's breakup, there has been a proliferation of long-distance carriers carrying both data and voice traffic, these still access the local central office for distribution. High-speed private backbones operated by companies such as Level 3, Global Crossing, AT&T, or MCI now compete to offer connectivity around the world, but as data travels from point to point, it inevitably passes from network to network through a handful of peering points, interconnection sites between networks that are, again, located in city cores. This further concentrates the network, privileges the bigger players, and increases the divide between a digital hub in the city core and the digital desert beyond.

[5] Janet Abbate, *Inventing the Internet* (Cambridge, MA: The MIT Press, 1999).

THE PALACE OF ETHER

In *Empire*, Antonio Negri and Michael Hardt describe the new world order created by the global spread of capital and communications technology, a transnational order that has emerged to supplant the bipolar era of the Cold War and the superpowers. With national governments withering away under the deterritorializing and liquefying forces of capitalism, Negri and Hardt claim that a new sovereignty is emerging. Like Baran's ideal system, this diffuse network of Empire supplants the old imperial model of center and periphery, replacing it with a placeless network of flows and hierarchies.

Empire is not ruled by one country, one people, or one place. Instead its force emanates from the global planetary network itself. Imperial sovereignty functions through three tiers that serve as checks and balances on each other while extending its power to all realms: monarchy, aristocracy, and democracy. These forms of sovereignty correspond to the Bomb (U. S. military superiority and nuclear supremacy), Money (the economic wealth of the G7), and Ether (the realm of the media, culture, and the global telecommunicational network). Although these tiers are placeless—any momentary fixities are quickly destabilized by the deterritorializing nature of Empire itself—Hardt and Negri suggest that "new Romes" appear to control them: Washington DC for the Bomb, New York for Money, and Los Angeles for Ether. [6]

Ether is the most historically advanced of these three forms of power. An anesthetic, Ether separates the mind from the body, and reduces the dominance of physical sensation while maintaining the consciousness of the patient. Under the spell of its influence, the most intimate and cherished of all physical space, that of the body itself, can be assaulted at will.

Los Angeles is the center of production for Ether. Hollywood, as both a mythic place and a mode of production, is the telematic inhaler for the rest

[6] Hardt and Negri, *Empire*, 347.

of the world, a sponge so soaked in Ether that it can anaesthetize the entire world. Now that we have Los Angeles, we no longer need other cities. Designed as a giant stage set, Los Angeles is always ready for broadcast. As a generic background, it can be exported to any location.

If Ether were to have a palace, it would have to be the 39-story One Wilshire tower in downtown Los Angeles. Constructed at the apogee of modernism by Skidmore, Owings, and Merrill, One Wilshire unequivocally declares that form follows function. Perhaps the worst building SOM ever designed, excusable only as a product of the provincial San Francisco office, One Wilshire appears to follow only two guiding principles. First, in order to create a visual identity, One Wilshire is designed as a skyscraper. Second, One Wilshire's window areas are maximized to provide light and views for the occupants. Throughout the design, expression of any form, including the expression of structure, is eliminated as superfluous. One Wilshire is a pure modernist building. Its neutral grid lacks symbolic content, making it a tower without qualities.

One Wilshire embodies the desire of the bourgeois metropolis to appear at all cost. Awkward in proportion and off-axis with regard to Wilshire boulevard, its only feature is height, incessantly affirming the value of the land beneath it. But this symbolic affirmation also helped ensure the building's obsolescence. In his 1971 essay "The Fluid Metropolis," Andrea Branzi observes that "the skyline becomes a diagram of the natural accumulation which has taken place of capital itself." Under late capitalism, he suggests, capital finally dominates "the empty space in which [it] expanded during its growth period." When "no reality exists any longer outside of the system," the skyscraper's representation of accumulation becomes obsolete. Branzi concludes that the horizontal factory and the supermarket—in which the circulation of information is made optimum and hierarchies disappear—would replace the tower as the foundational typologies for the fluid metropolis. [7]

Since then, Branzi's prophecy has been fulfilled. Communication replaces accumulation. The increasingly horizontal corporation, organized along Taylorist and cybernetic principles of communicational efficiency, constructs low, spreading buildings for its offices in the suburbs. Damaged by the decentralizing policies of Cold War urbanism and increasingly threatened by the sprawling suburbs, the congested vertical urban core began to empty in the 1970s. One Wilshire's once beneficial vertical signification of "office building" and "valuable real estate" began to get in the way of its own economic sustainability. By the mid-1980s, the regime of horizontality was firmly in place and One Wilshire was obsolete.

Eventually, however, a new opportunity presented itself and One Wilshire's height returned to its advantage. With the deregulation of the telecommunications industry, long distance carrier MCI, which had its own nationwide microwave network, required a tall structure on which to install microwave antennas in close proximity to the AT&T (formerly SBC, prior to that PacBell, before that AT&T) central switching station at 400 South Grand Street downtown. Although as a condition of deregulation, competing long distance carriers are, by law, allowed access to the lines at the central

[7] Archizoom Associates, "No-Stop City. Residential Parkings. Climatic Universal Sistem," *Domus* 496, March 1971, 49-55.

switching station, AT&T does not have to provide them with space for their equipment. Only three thousand feet from the central switching station and at the time one of the tallest buildings downtown, One Wilshire was ideal for MCI. Seeing a friendly environment close to the central switching station, other long-distance carriers, Internet service providers, and networking companies began to install their equipment at One Wilshire.

Soon, however, carriers turned to fiber optic technology, glass light-bearing strands that can carry multiple data streams simultaneously. As fiber technology has become the primary means of carrying telecommunications traffic, the microwave towers on top have dwindled in importance—they are now used by Verizon for connection to its cell phone network. With One Wilshire's proximity to the coast and cable landing stations in the Santa Barbara and Ventura areas, a good portion of transpacific traffic from the Americas—and even Europe—flows through One Wilshire. As a consequence, One Wilshire is not only a staging ground for carriers connecting to the local system, it is a key peer-to-peer connection point. In the fourth floor Meet Me Room, telecom providers are allowed to run interconnects directly between each other without charge. By creating direct connections between each other's lines in the structure, telecom providers avoid charges imposed by linking through a third-party hub. The result is a dramatic cost savings for the companies, allowing One Wilshire's management to charge $250 per square foot per month in the Meet Me Room, the highest per-square-foot rent on the North American continent.

Because space in One Wilshire is at such a premium, companies run conduit to adjacent structures. Over a dozen nearby buildings have been converted to such telecom hotels, providing bases to telephone and Internet companies seeking locations near the fountain of data at One Wilshire. This centralization of information defies predictions that the Internet and new technologies will undo cities. But neither does it lead to a revival of

downtown in classical terms. The buildings around One Wilshire are valuable again, but largely uninhabited. Ironically, if one of the reasons for the downfall of the American downtown is the slowdown in transportation and wear on infrastructure created by congestion, the emptiness of the streets in Los Angeles's telecom district ensures that this will never again be a problem for this neighborhood.

One Wilshire stands as a continuous demonstration of the phases of the metropolis and the current state of the postmetropolitan realm. One Wilshire proves that the new functions of the city do not need a shape of their own but rather are repelled by that possibility. Physical form is secondary today. The transformation that One Wilshire undergoes from its construction in 1966 to the present parallels the transition from material reality to virtual

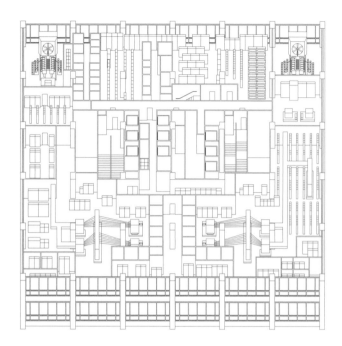

reality, from Cold War to Empire. With the full development of the postmet-ropolitan realm and the corresponding global saturation of material produc-tion, we enter the world of immaterial culture.

The virtual is generally perceived as a drive against the spatial or phys-ical world. Nevertheless, as One Wilshire demonstrates, the virtual world requires an infrastructure that exists in the physical and spatial world. Though Ether is formless, it has to be created. Its production requires an enormous amount of physical hardware and consistent expertise. Because of this, Ether is produced in places such as Hollywood studios, locations where highly skilled technicians can meet and collect around cameras and computers. Massive telecommunicational hubs like One Wilshire and their radial networks make the virtual world possible, and firmly ground it into the concrete cityscape. Once this raw data of Ether is created, it has to be stored and organized through stable control centers. These control centers, filled with row after row of servers, generate an enormous amount of heat and require vast cooling systems with multiple back-up power units in order to function without interruption. Constant monitoring of these systems is vital as interruptions affect the entire system. Once the data has been collected, it has to be distributed outside of the building. Fiber optic cable, currently the most effective way of transmitting large quantities of data out of the building into the rest of the world, is expensive to lay and requires a significant negotiations to secure rights-of-way. Most telecommunication companies cannot afford all of these investments individually and so pool their resources at a single location providing connectivity close to the transmission source. Through One Wilshire, virtually all of the global market leaders share a physical investment on the West coast. Being "plugged in" is their literal need, not just an abstract notion. Because One Wilshire is tied to this physical location, it undermines the concept of an autonomous virtuality, revealing instead the simultaneous importance and abandonment of the physical world.

No matter how banal, One Wilshire is the product of modernism and through its curtain wall grid, partakes in the movement's blanket promise to deliver democracy through technology, visibility, and neutrality. Founded on visual spectacles such as testimony, the Senate, the Parliament, the inauguration oath, the Pledge of Allegiance, and the State of the Union address, democracy takes place in public, in the street, in the agora, and in the newspaper. In contrast, the clandestine, the shady, and the back-room deal are the realm of corrupt politicians and the theater for cynical reason.

Advocates of modern architecture proclaimed that a culture of brick prevented democracy from functioning and proposed translucent or transparent glass as a means by which to produce political transparency. In his 1914 book *Glasarchitektur* theorist Paul Scheerbart declared "Colored glass destroys hatred" while in his 1926-27 competition entry for the Palace of the League of Nations, Bauhaus director Hannes Meyer proposed a neutral and transparent glass grid with exposed stairwells to prevent the making of covert deals. [8] During the Cold War, Western governments, eager to demonstrate their allegiance to democracy, adopted International Style modernism to signify democratic action, even if that signification dissimulated what really happened in the grid. The recognition of the dark qualities of modern democracy—the revelation of the Pentagon papers, widespread domestic surveillance, Nixon's Dirty Tricks and Watergate—accompanied the collapse of modernism in the 1970s. [9]

If One Wilshire promises transparency through its glass façade, the same is often said of the glass fiber optic network that fills it. Proponents of the so-called "Californian Ideology"—largely based in the Bay Area, not in Los Angeles—suggest that the convergence of media, computing, and telecommunications will result in a new world of electronic transparency with near perfect knowledge, spirited debate outside the media machine, and participatory democracy of a libertarian bent for everyone. [10] But just as the façades of International Style modernism dissimulated invisible dealings within, the fiber optic net's presence does not reveal what passes through it. The privatization of the Internet and global communications networks have made them unknowable. The flow of telecommunications today is classified property, a question of corporate intelligence. The recent attempt by geographers to create an

[8] On the glass façade, see Janet Ward, *Weimar Surfaces. Urban Visual Culture in 1920s Germany* (Berkeley: University of California Press, 2001), 41-91.

[9] On the adoption of modern architecture by the United States government, see Lois Craig, *The Federal Presence* (Cambridge, MA: MIT Press, 1978).

[10] Richard Barbrook and Andy Cameron, "The Californian Ideology," *Mute* (3). Available: http://www.alamut.com/subj/ideologies/pessimism/califIdeo_I.html

Atlas of Cyberspace concluded that the privatization of the Internet and modern telecommunications have made the dominant forms of contemporary space fundamentally unmappable. This corresponds to Fredric Jameson's thesis that since late capitalism is total and lacks any exterior, it is impossible for the subject to understand his or her position in the system. We can make cognitive maps—indeed, Jameson suggests, that is our task—but they must be incomplete and imperfect. The promise of a world of clarity and transparency is undone by the reality that modern telecommunications constitute a web that refuses to become visible. Yet again the modern tries for the transparent through technology, yet again it fails. "

Ours is an unmappable, unknowable world that disappears into a mysterious global network of capital and connections. So it is at One Wilshire. In September 2001, CRG-West, an operating partner of the Carlyle Group, acquired the building from the Paramount Group, a real estate investment firm owned by Otto Versand, a Hamburg-based concern specializing in retail clothing, mail order catalogues, and the Internet. Paramount Group owned the structure for some 25 years, but One Wilshire's new owner is more appropriate for the Palace of Ether. The Carlyle Group is named after New York City's Carlyle Hotel, the building where the firm was established, which in turn was named after Thomas Carlyle, the Scottish essayist and historian. In his 1832 *Sartor Resartus*, Carlyle created a new kind of book that blended fact and fiction, speculation and history, essay and satire while confronting the question of truth in a rapidly industrializing society that was losing its religious faith. Finding only contempt for humanity, Carlyle's narrator ponders the "Everlasting No" of refusal, passes through the "Center of Indifference," and eventually embraces the "Everlasting Yea." In later writings, Carlyle

11 Fredric Jameson, "Postmodernism, or the Cultural Logic of Late Capitalism," *New Left Review* 146 (July/August 1984): 53-92 and Robin Kitchin and Martin Dodge, *Atlas of Cyberspace* (London: Pearson, 2001).

attacked laissez-faire capitalism for its destruction of communal values and promotion of individualism as well as what he called the "dismal science" of economics. Indicting aristocracy as deadening and democracy as nonsense, Carlyle called for heroic leadership instead, but his reputation would be tarnished after his notorious essay of 1849, an "An Occasional Discourse on the Nigger Question," in which he defended slavery as a means of keeping lazy people busy at work. During the twentieth century, fascist leaders would admire Carlyle. Adolf Hitler is reputed to have read Carlyle's biography of Frederick the Great during his last days in the Berlin bunker.

For its part, the Carlyle Group is a private global investment firm specializing in buyouts of assets in real estate and defense. Founded to take advantage of a tax loophole in which Alaskan Eskimos could sell losses at a discount to corporations that, in turn, would claim the full loss as a credit on their taxes—a process that often involved exaggerating the losses of the Eskimos—in the early 1990s the Carlyle Group turned its initial winnings into a quick fortune by buying up defense contractors whose stock was laid low by defense cutbacks in the aftermath of the fall of the Berlin Wall.

Founded in the capital of Money, owners of the palace of Ether, the Carlyle Group is based in the capital of the Bomb. Unlike most equity firms Carlyle locates its headquarters in Washington DC instead of New York, more precisely on Pennsylvania Avenue, half way between the White House and the Capitol building. Throughout its two decades of existence, Carlyle has excelled at exploiting its relationships with the government, leading *The New Republic* magazine to dub the firm "the Access Capitalists." The list of personnel who have worked for, or advised, Carlyle includes luminaries from U. S. administrations past and present such as former Secretary of State Jim Baker, former Secretary of Defense Frank Carlucci, former White House budget director Richard Darman, former FCC chairman William Kennard, former SEC chairman Arthur Levitt, former President George H. W. Bush as well as international figures such as former British Prime Minister John Major, former Philippines President Fidel Ramos, and financier George Soros.

As the attacks of the morning of September 11, 2001 unfolded, the Carlyle Group was holding its annual international investor conference at the Ritz-Carlton hotel in Washington. Carlucci, Baker, and Bush attended the meeting, as did a number of the Group's key foreign investors, including Shafiq bin Laden, Osama bin Laden's estranged half-brother, there to represent his family. With the revelation that Osama bin Laden was behind the attacks, the bin Laden family liquidated its stake to quell the growing public perception of a conflict of interest regarding their investment in a key defense contractor that would profit from the chase for their relation. [12]

[12] Dan Briody. *The Iron Triangle. Inside The Secret World of the Carlyle Group* (New York: John Wiley and Sons, 2003).

How, precisely, One Wilshire fits into the Carlyle Group's strategy is not clear, but three possible strategies seem likely. First, if One Wilshire's importance is due to its role as a key peering point, telecoms using it as a base for their Los Angeles switches still need access to AT&T's local lines. Although AT&T is a competitor to these carriers, it has also previously been an ally of the Carlyle group, pointing to a synergistic relationship. Second, Carlyle is adept at profit from its access to the federal government. With telecommunications bills being rapidly re-written in the United States Congress, the group is strategically positioned to benefit. Third, the huge amount of foreign and domestic traffic flowing through One Wilshire offers a signal opportunity for the American government, which was recently revealed to be installing electronic eavesdropping equipment at telecommunications facilities without search warrants. [13]

Los Angeles is the capital of Ether but the rhizomatic tendrils of Ether extend across the world, dominating it with its silent outposts. Like One Wilshire, carrier hotels, telecom hotels, data hotels, carrier neutral collocation facilities, exchanges, and switching stations are generally found in the densest part of a city or its financial district. In Los Angeles, Ether is concentrated in one area and largely even in one building. By contrast, in New York, Ether is dispersed: there are some half dozen buildings devoted largely to telecommunications in Manhattan. For example, 32 Avenue of the Americas is typical of a building design for telecommunications that has recently been retrofitted as a collocation facility. Designed by Ralph Walker and built in 1932, 32 Avenue of the Americas once housed AT&T's offices and equipment for transatlantic communications, but has recently been remodeled by Tyco International to serve as the New York TelExchange Center. Tenants are encouraged to take advantage of Tyco's transatlantic fiber optic network,

[13] Eric Lichtblau and James Risen, "Spy Agency Mined Vast Data Trove, Officials Report," *The New York Times*, December 24, 2005, 1.

which terminates here. Another model can be seen at the AT&T Long Lines Building at 33 Thomas Street, designed by John Carl Warnecke & Associates and built in 1974. Clad in pink Swedish granite, the Long Lines Building was built to resist nuclear blast and fallout and to operate self-sufficiently for two weeks after attack. Each floor is 6 meters in height, providing room for AT&T's equipment. Unlike One Wilshire or 32 Avenue of the Americas, this facility is only for AT&T, the largest telecommunications company in the United States.

IMMATERIAL CULTURE

For the most part, One Wilshire is an ugly and ordinary building, akin to the now classic postmodernist retirement home designed by Robert Venturi and Denise Scott Brown, Guild House. In designing Guild House, the architects decided to avoid the monumental and instead build a structure more appropriate to the banal demands of modern life. Cut-rate detailing and low-cost prefabricated elements made Guild House a stark reminder that modernism won its battle not because of ideology but because it was cheaper to build than neoclassicism. Projects by the firm that followed this methodology would be condemned as "ugly and ordinary" by Skidmore Owings and Merrill's lead designer Gordon Bunshaft. In response Venturi and Brown adopted Bunshaft's term of derision as a virtue. Choosing to strike preemptively against the ill-suited signage that clients inevitably put atop modernist buildings, Venturi and Scott Brown added their own sign to announce the structure's name: a second-rate panel that simply states "Guild House" above the entrance. At the top of the building the architects also mounted a non-functioning, gold anodized antenna to denote the building's common room and signify that the elderly watch a lot of TV. Seen by both critics and occupants as a cynical joke at the expense of the inhabitants, this useless antenna was later removed. The loss of the antenna was not, however, a fatal blow. Venturi and Scott Brown observed that the ability to remove or replace signage at will gave flexibility to structures. Upon returning from a research trip to Las Vegas, the architects coined the term "the decorated shed" to refer to a modernist universal space coupled with a sign. Developed by Venturi and Scott Brown specifically to address the needs of a democratic information society, the decorated shed could change its function and meaning at will. Although Guild House is held by many to be a key building in the evolution of postmodernism, the ideas of the decorated shed and ugly and ordinary architecture proved too controversial for even the most avant-garde architects and Venturi and Scott Brown were virtually ostracized from the profession. [14]

Like Guild House, One Wilshire is simply a neutral shell lacking any aesthetic gestures. There is no reason to think that Bunshaft wouldn't have called One Wilshire "ugly and ordinary" as well. It was constructed at almost the same time as Guild House and shares many of its features. Unlike the AT&T Long Lines building, which Venturi and Scott Brown would have classified as a duck for possessing a form indissociable from its function, One Wilshire is a decorated shed. It has its own second-rate sign: banal modernist lettering across its façade announces "One Wilshire" to the rest of the city. Although the antennas at One Wilshire originally had a purpose, they are now just as superfluous as the ornament once crowning Guild House, empty symbols of a retired modern technology. But One Wilshire goes a step further than the decorated shed: its signage is obsolete from the start. It will never need to be removed. The building's real address has never been One Wilshire, but rather 624 South Grand. An unbridgeable gap between signifier and signified, between form and function, opens up at One Wilshire. The fact that this architecturally meritless structure is also the most valuable real estate in North America only confirms that the role of the building as a producer of effect or meaning is obsolete.

Where Guild House was a home for the elderly, One Wilshire is the home in which we dwell telematically. Just as the elderly watched television in Guild House as a way of checking out of the weariness of life, we check into the global space of telecommunications in order to escape the dead world of objects. In both cases, however, the desire is to leave behind this world of material goods for something more pure, to escape our responsibility to objects by submitting to something greater. Managers of progressive nursing

[14] Robert Venturi, Denise Scott Brown, and Steven Izenour, "Ugly and Ordinary Architecture, or the Decorated Shed," in *Learning from Las Vegas*, revised edition (Cambridge, MA: The MIT Press, 1977), 87-163.

homes today understand that this is part of our lives, often requiring that residents divest themselves of both financial and physical assets in order to better facilitate their care.

The objects produced during the 1970s and 1980s were largely throwaway novelty goods and fashions and are transitional objects on the way toward immaterial culture. Real things give themselves up too easily, they are quickly known and classified. Like potential lovers, once they are purchased, objects become dead to our desires, lifeless pieces of junk. They are items for a fractured marketplace, without group needs or identities. Communication technology has also changed the way people interact, creating a form of culture devoid of material references. Cell phone conversations, MP3 players, and the Internet all offer an alternative to consumer goods. The telecommunicational realm promises that the spirit can finally part from flesh and exist fully in a world of electronic images. These images are seductive because, circulating endlessly in an ethereal world, they cannot be possessed. We can fantasize about having such images to no end without ever feeling the disappointing responsibility of ownership.

Before late capitalism, objects had meaning because they were necessary but scarce. In our affluent society, however, objects are overabundant, becoming merely components within a system of exchange without any clear

use-value to determine their price. The very basis of late capitalism presupposes the delinking of currencies from the gold standard or any other guarantor of value. Today money proliferates wildly even as it means nothing. There is no longer a clear logic to the system of capital. The dot-com boom, beanie babies, and vastly inflated real estate values are all based on mass delusion. Value itself does not come out of any deeper truth but is constructed by temporary notions and mass delusions.

Within immaterial culture, consumer goods lose their natural meaning and become fully abstracted as empty forms, ready to be filled with a variety of meanings that we apply to them depending on context. Immaterial culture makes possible a system of consumption beyond cynical reason in which even the most sinister or foul objects can be desirable. All objects are now wild signs, free-floating signifiers unable to represent anything specific themselves, part of the mechanism of circulation, which has become a goal in and of itself. Money, as Hal Foster observes, purportedly the guarantor of value, is the ultimate wild sign. Gold is locked away at Fort Knox, too heavy to move. Instead, the value of currency is tied merely to abstraction and desire. With nothing underwriting it except Derridean *différance*, the economy is sustained only because of the continued inevitability of circulation in the network. [15]

This is a defensive measure for capital, so that massive run-ups in markets and unprecedented collapses can occur without any real consequence. The increasing role of telecommunications and computers in everyday life does not do away with objects. Far from it, in immaterial culture physical objects proliferate endlessly. As the logic of our daily lives becomes more and more removed from the direct consequences of our actions, objects are marketed and sold for their symbolic values alone. A teapot by Phillipe

[15] Hal Foster, "Wild Signs: The Breakup of the Sign in Seventies Art," in John Tagg, ed. *The Cultural Politics of 'Postmodernism'*, (Binghamton: Department of Art and Art History, State University of New York at Binghamton, 1989), 69-86.

Starck costs more than a regular teapot because of its styling, even though it doesn't really work. But the styling doesn't really matter either, only the name of Starck as a marker of value. Physical objects carry economic value only at moments of exchange: the moment they become so desirable that you want to purchase them and the moment that you can no longer tolerate their presence and want to get rid of them.

We still feel the need to own objects, even if the gratitude of ownership is fleeting. The on-again and off-again emotions we have about our objects confuse us, leaving us bewildered and lost. Physical objects will always ultimately repel us because they cannot satisfy our desire for self-negation, our desire to lose ourselves in their world. So it is that our love for objects is routinely replaced by a deep hate. The dream of immaterial culture is revenge on the world of objects, but it remains only a dream. We sell our possessions relentlessly on eBay but still they accumulate, contributing nothing to our lives. Every day more debt, more things, less joy.

We will never find a release from the need to own. Even if we can't sustain the gratitude of ownership, we purchase goods to validate our identity and diversity as individuals existing outside of this media web. But more than that, in submitting ourselves as willing slaves to our world of useless objects, we hope to become as disposable to them as they are to us today. If, unlike Berliner-Mauer, we cannot join their world, we dream of a new equality: being as ethereal and meaningless to them as they are to us. We pray for dispensation, to leave this material world and dissipate in Ether. And yet, as conflicted beings, we also hope that one day our objects will invest in us the same animistic beliefs with which we invest them. This is not our nightmare, it is the achievement of an Utopian dream, presence without purpose or responsibility: a slacker response of ambivalence and helplessness.

But in the transition from material to immaterial culture not only have none of the physical elements of society changed, it is now clear they will never need to be changed again. Just as fiction disappears into reality, so too, the new has been absorbed into present. Over a decade ago, Ridley Scott stated that if he had to shoot Blade Runner again, he would simply point the camera down a street in Los Angeles, perhaps in front of One Wilshire. One of the most advanced science fiction stories of our day—the Matrix trilogy—projects a future superficially identical to the present day. If the present is indistinguishable from the future, Wallpaper* Magazine, the Eames La Chaise, the newest models of the Mazda Miata, Cooper Mini, Camaro, Ford GTS, and Ford Thunderbird demonstrate that the past only comes to perfection in the present. Retrofitted, One Wilshire is far greater than anything it ever was.

Just as One Wilshire was recycled into a citadel for immaterial culture, all we can do is recycle old things in phases to make them newly desirable commodities again. Supply and demand emerge out of what is already lying around. The metropolis is complete. Only our relationship to the elements of the world around us is freed of permanence and keeps moving.

Although nothing has a universal meaning or a lasting value, objects still convey provisional meanings and attain temporary values created on the fly, often for very short durations. For a month a Beanie Baby is worth $1,000. The next month it is worth $3 again. This doesn't mean that anything goes. Objects can still only function within a system. Like tech stocks, the empty promise of objects is precisely what allows them to remain vital. There is no longer a fixed natural state of identity or being. All that is left is desire and the craving for its impossible satisfaction.

Value is now a commodity in and of itself, regularly sought out and consumed. All objects and all people are members of a giant stock exchange, not investors on the floor, but rather flickering numbers running across a banner, some rising, some falling, always moving up and down. Individuals long to become virtual and escape into Ether. It is through this physical apparatus that Hollywood stars, celebrities, and criminals obtain another body, a media life. Neither sacred nor living, this media life is pure image, more consistent and dependable than physical life itself. It is the dream we all share: that we might become objects, or better yet, lose our corporeality to become pure images.

Few objects demonstrate the drive to become media as does the 12" single "Blue Monday." The New Wave band New Order began as Joy Division, a British Punk group that starkly embodied the post-industrial alienation of late 1970s Manchester and whose history culminated in the suicide of its lead singer Ian Curtis on the eve of their first North American tour. Rising from the ashes of Joy Division, New Order embraced synthesizer technology (generally considered soulless by the Punks) and rejected the clamor of Punk for the beat of the dance floor. In "Blue Monday," the band achieved phenomenal media success, creating the most popular single of all time. But in their desire to become more digital—and hence more immaterial—than actually possible at the time, New Order retained graphic designer Neville Brody to make a die cut cover that would resemble the sleeve of a large floppy disk. The unique look won critical acclaim, but according to legend the most popular 12" of all time cost the band 20 cents for every copy sold, ruining them financially but assuring their place in the regime of media.

Media life promises eternal existence, cleansed of unscripted character flaws and accidents—a guaranteed legacy that defies aging and death by already appearing dead on arrival. The idols of millions via magazines, film, and television are disembodied, lifeless forms without content or meaning. But the terrifying truth is that, although a media image may last forever, like Michael Jackson, its host is prone to destruction and degradation. Data itself is not free of physicality. When it is reduplicated or backed up to file and stored via a remote host it suffers the same limitations as the physical world. It can be erased, lost, and compromised. The constant frustration of

CDs, DVDs, and hard drives is that they disintegrate. Up to 20% of the information carefully collected on Jet Propulsion Laboratory computers during NASA's 1976 Viking mission to Mars has been lost. The average Web page lasts only a hundred days, the typical life span of a flea on a dog. Even if data isn't lost, the ability to read it soon disappears. Photos of the Amazon Basin taken by satellites in the 1970s are critical to understanding long-term trends in deforestation but are trapped forever on indecipherable magnetic tapes. This resistance by the physical aspect of virtuality to its immaterial perfection is what keeps us plugged in. It is the crash of data, like an earthquake or tsunami, that reminds us of our own limitations and momentarily returns purpose and value to our lives.

That the dot-com and telecom busts occurred in the first year of the new millennium is no accident. Those who participated and invested in these busts did not do so without reason. Like the followers of the Heaven's Gate cult and those who hoped that the year 2000—or better yet, a Kubrick-esque 2001—would mark the end of all things, they were just desperate to believe that the end was near. The process of investing in Pets.com was a matter of giving oneself up. Borrowing on margin to invest not only the entirety of one's pension in Akamai or Worldcom but to generate a life-crushing debt as a byproduct as well is voluntary slavery.

The pundits were mistaken: it was not that we all hoped to take our profits and get out of the boom before it failed, it was that we wanted to be part of its failure and to feel its destruction. Like the Bomb, the greatest disappointment of the dot-com crash of 2000 was its failure to bring about its greatest promise: the end of all things.

Today members of the architectural post-avant-garde maintain that architecture should do nothing more than embody the flows of capital. Instead of enslaving itself to capital, as it does now, and instead of fulfilling the master-slave dialectic to become capital's master, as it always wished to be under modernism, architecture now decides to end the game and achieve oneness with capital. [16]

But if achieving a state of oneness with capital is architecture's fantasy, what better place for this to happen than at One Wilshire? To become capital, architecture must first become Ether. Architecture, like all other objects, will lose its intrinsic value and enter into a pure system of exchange. Through symbol libraries and the magic of the .dxf import command, it has become possible for architectural plans to reproduce at will. The restrooms from Frank Gehry's signature building, the Guggenheim Museum at Bilbao, can be copied onto a flash drive by an intern to endlessly re-appear in schools of architecture worldwide, their first role in life irrelevant and forgotten. In this light, the prevalence of the computation-intensive blob in the academy is revealed as the product of fear, a desperate attempt to reintroduce the hand and slow down architectural production just at the moment that it threatens to proliferate wildly, becoming pure Ether.

One Wilshire has no such fear. Created before the dawn of computer-aided design, it transcends architecture as pure diagram and pure Idea. Endlessly repeatable, there is no limit to its potent reach. It is the architectural realization of Hegel's Spirit itself. One Wilshire is an architecture of pure self-negation, simultaneously real and virtual, visible and unseen. One Wilshire is an unimportant building without any physical presence or ability to signify its function. Yet it is crucial. One Wilshire is the unreal exposing and making real of the unreal. One Wilshire is the palace for the empire of Ether.

[16] Rem Koolhaas in *Rem Koolhaas: Conversations With Students, Architecture at Rice University; 30* (New York: Princeton Architectural Press, 1996), 64.

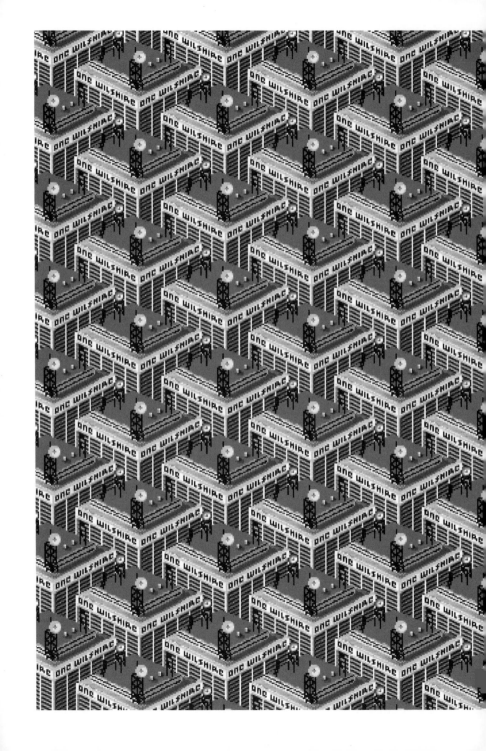

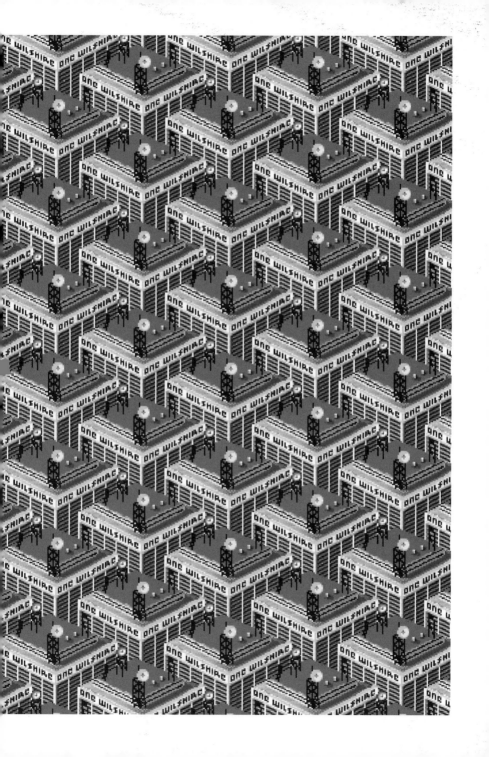

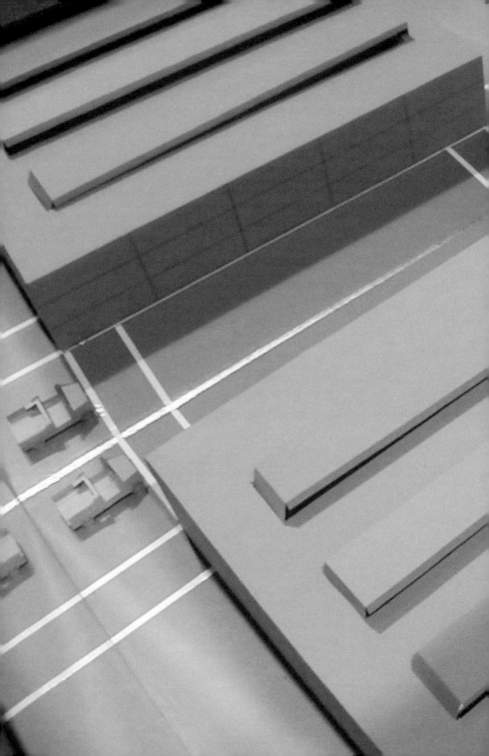

ETHICS

VOLUNTARY SLAVERY
THE STIMULUS PROGRESSION:
Muzak

VOLUNTARY SLAVERY

Collectors are fanatics, often sacrificing their lives for their collections. The average serious record collector owns somewhere between 10,000 and 100,000 disks. Owning this much vinyl necessitates devoting an enormous amount of time, money, and personal space to inert, toxic objects. In an extreme collector's home, records fill the cabinets, block the refrigerator, stack in the bathroom and pile along the stairs. One Long Island collector named Clarence A. Browne boasted an almost unimaginable selection of approximately three-quarters of a million records—measuring in at somewhere around seven thousand, eight hundred cubic feet of vinyl. Clarence allowed his obsession with records to reach life-threatening levels. Once owning a fourteen room mansion and sizable assets, he squandered everything in order to maintain his collection, an obsession that he would put before everything else including heat, a working kitchen, and personal comfort. [1]

Clarence's devotion to his record collection did not come from the value of the information recorded on the discs. On the contrary, Clarence would collect almost any record. Neither did it come from a sense of nostalgia for the music on the disks—Clarence owned far more records than he could have actually played or experienced during his lifetime. Nor was it out of a need to construct

---

[1] Evan Eisenberg, *Recording Angel, Explorations in Phonography* (New York: McGraw Hill, 1987), 1-9. Also see Irvin Molotsky, "A Penniless Heir Fears for His Record Collection," *The New York Times*, February 1, 1978, B1, B9.

a hermetically sealed world of order into which he could escape—Clarence often gifted his most prized pieces to friends and strangers alike. Instead, Clarence's desire for records and his urge to over-collect came from a drive to give himself up to the world of objects.

Jean Baudrillard helps us understand that collecting is the product of the way that consumer goods operate as a language ordering contemporary society. Baudrillard observes that in the system of objects we have constructed, objects no longer need to communicate with or serve us, they simply relate to each other, and in so doing instruct us as to how they should be handled. Like all other consumer goods, records no longer need us. They form a self-contained world that can only be sorted and organized over and over again. [2]

But why collect? According to Sigmund Freud, "the passion to possess" is the product of toilet training. As parents first teach their children to use the toilet, they force them to move from a world ordered by the timing and pleasure of their own bodily functions, to one of abstract time and scheduled labor. If bodily waste, a gift to the child's parents, is removed before the child is ready, the child may feel not only that the object of their labor is disgusting and inappropriate to enjoy, he or she may be lead to believe that their life has no real purpose, that it is only an abstract system by which meaningless labor is produced. Freud believed that some individuals, thoroughly traumatized by this process, derive their primary sensual pleasure from retaining objects. The association this

[2] Jean Baudrillard, *The System of Objects* (London: Verso, 1996), 87-89.

relentless collecting has with feces forces them into a simultaneous sense of pride and guilt over their collections. Collectors understand that without the need to labor, life itself can have no authentic purpose and, running up against the relative ease of life in an affluent society, comfort themselves by laboring for an objectal Other. By devoting their lives to collections, collectors makes themselves important. Only by suffering for the object do collectors become human. [3]

Like Job (or Ayub in the Qur'an), record collectors endure great adversity, endlessly laboring and suffering to prove themselves worthy to their collections. It is this determination to believe in and devote yourself to something with no intrinsic value that unites religion and consumerism alike. Like religions, records are outmoded and outdated. Moreover, with the spread of tele-communicational networks, even the concept of the collection is ludicrous. As mass-produced consumer goods openly traded on eBay or GEMM.com, only a select few disks are not readily available from some distributor given minimal searching. MP3s and other digital audio formats undo scarcity, allowing the rarest track to be reproduced exactly and infinitely. The most collectible records are often rare pressings that can be identified not by any distinguishing marks on the cover or any sonic characteristics, but rather by cryptic notes inscribed on the vinyl matrix next to the label.

3 Sigmund Freud, *The Standard Edition of the Complete Psychological Works of Sigmund Freud*, trans. James Strachey (London: Hogarth Press, 1971), vol. 7, 12 and vol. 23, 259-260.

Collectors submit themselves to voluntary slavery, an action not innocent but rather of staggering consequence at a time in which some twenty-seven million people are actually enslaved in places across the world such as Africa, India, and Southeast Asia, as well as in the United States and Europe. [4] These individuals are subject to complete deprivation of freedom either through violence or through indentured servitude. Never before have so many been enslaved and never before has slavery been so forgotten. But is it possible that the tacit acceptance of slavery today is due to a broader condition of enslavement spreading throughout culture as a consequence of Empire?

Only the most naïve might think of the contemporary subject as truly free. We are all masters and slaves. The establishment wishes us to think of ourselves only as masters of the world. This is literally true for many: the number of individuals owning stocks is at an all-time high. The restructuring of pension plans to allow employees direct choice within the stock market, the growth in profit-sharing, together with the explosion of choice in individual investment, makes us all capitalists. We are even told to look forward to the privatization of the Social Security program to allow individuals to invest their contributions on Wall Street. The result is that more people than ever before share in the wealth created by exploiting the labor of others. But our role as masters only underscores our role as slaves. It is not merely others who are exploited; after all, they are likely to own stock too. Never have our jobs been less secure.

[4] Kevin Bales, *Disposable People. New Slavery in the Global Economy* (Berkeley: University of California Press, 1999), 23.

The corporation's responsibility to shareholders—who are, after all, people similar to us, or perhaps, through profit-sharing, are quite literally ourselves—means that layoffs are a constant threat. And never has the workplace been so cutthroat: who does not live in fear that one's superiors—or underlings!—will decide that this is the day to call one's bluff? Coupled with this vertiginous lack of job certainty is the direct enslavement we suffer to others through debt. Between student loans, mortgages, automobile loans, and credit cards, personal debt is at an all-time high. And with the world thoroughly capitalized, there is no refuge to avoid enslavement. Under late capitalism, art, emotion, and sex are first and foremost sources of profit, thereby subject to its inexorable laws.

Neither can we turn to Marxism. Not only has it been colonized for profit wherever possible, the analytic model developed under Marxism runs aground against this new blurring of identities. Marx's analysis depended on clear distinctions between bourgeoisie (slaver) and proletariat (slave). Today, however our complicity in the system is total. We are each other's masters; we enslave ourselves. To that, Marxism's critique has no answer. Yet while Marxism fails us as a means of analysis, the unpredictable swiftness of actually existing Communism's collapse in the East Block a decade ago demonstrates the possibility of self-awakening and liberation within individuals. Once the populace understood they were enslaving themselves, the bleak regimes controlling them of their own invention, they stopped believing in them. Communism collapsed overnight and the Berlin Wall fell.

To explain, we need to revisit Hegel's dialectic of the master and the slave. In this narrative, two individuals confront each other. In so doing, each comes to an awareness of his or herself by seeing how the other perceives them. As a result of the encounter, one individual becomes dominant, the master, and enslaves the other. The master comes to think of the slave as a mere tool to be used, a deficient self, living only to satisfy the master's needs. In time, however, the master grows dependent on the slave, relying on him or her for every need. Meanwhile the slave, depending only upon his or her own wits and skill, slowly frees himself or herself from any dependency on the master. Even if in shackles, the slave comes to understand that the work he or she does affirms his or her nature as an individual. Lacking that affirmation, the master winds up empty, without identity. [5]

Bono, the world-famous recording artist and human rights activist, once stated, "Death begins in your record collection." This is not a death sentence, but a warning. If today we are both masters and slaves, it is only through realizing that we simultaneously occupy those dual roles that we free ourselves. Only when we understand that we create not freedom but our own alienation and enslavement can we move forward.

The love that record collectors like Clarence feel for vinyl is not abstract. It is a form of voluntary slavery. Obsessive record collectors understand their disks are the excreta and memory of living beings and as such contain traces

---

[5] Leo Rauch, David Sherman, and Georg Wilhelm Friedrich Hegel, *Hegel's Phenomenology of the Self: Text and Commentary* (Albany: State University of New York Press, 1999), 26-27.

of souls hidden in their grooves—this is a promise that is maintained even if a record is never played. The sense of mastery that record collectors find within their collections bridges the most apparent aspect of contemporary culture, the absoluteness of quantification, with its most absent quality, an almost incommunicable personal meaning. Records are collected in order to create an ideal catalogue of friends. Etymologically they "count down" the time to an impossibly complete and perfect scale model of the world. The ideal collection literally promises to provide the world itself as a goal, yet remains elusive enough to become impossible to acquire. This is the seduction of the collection, it offers an end that cannot ever be met but that instead continually compels collectors to move forward. Collections transform the world of goods into a world of fetish. Stripping any traces of function or practicality from the items in their collections, collectors desperately try to return the pieces back to a symbolic world of transcendence and meaning through their own self-sacrifice as well as by constructing their own, personally symbolic order of the system of objects. Ultimately, the more they collect, the more impractical the maintenance and nurturing of the collection becomes. The more the collection demands of their attention, actively fighting their ability to live, the more magical and meaningful it makes their lives.

THE STIMULUS PROGRESSION: Muzak

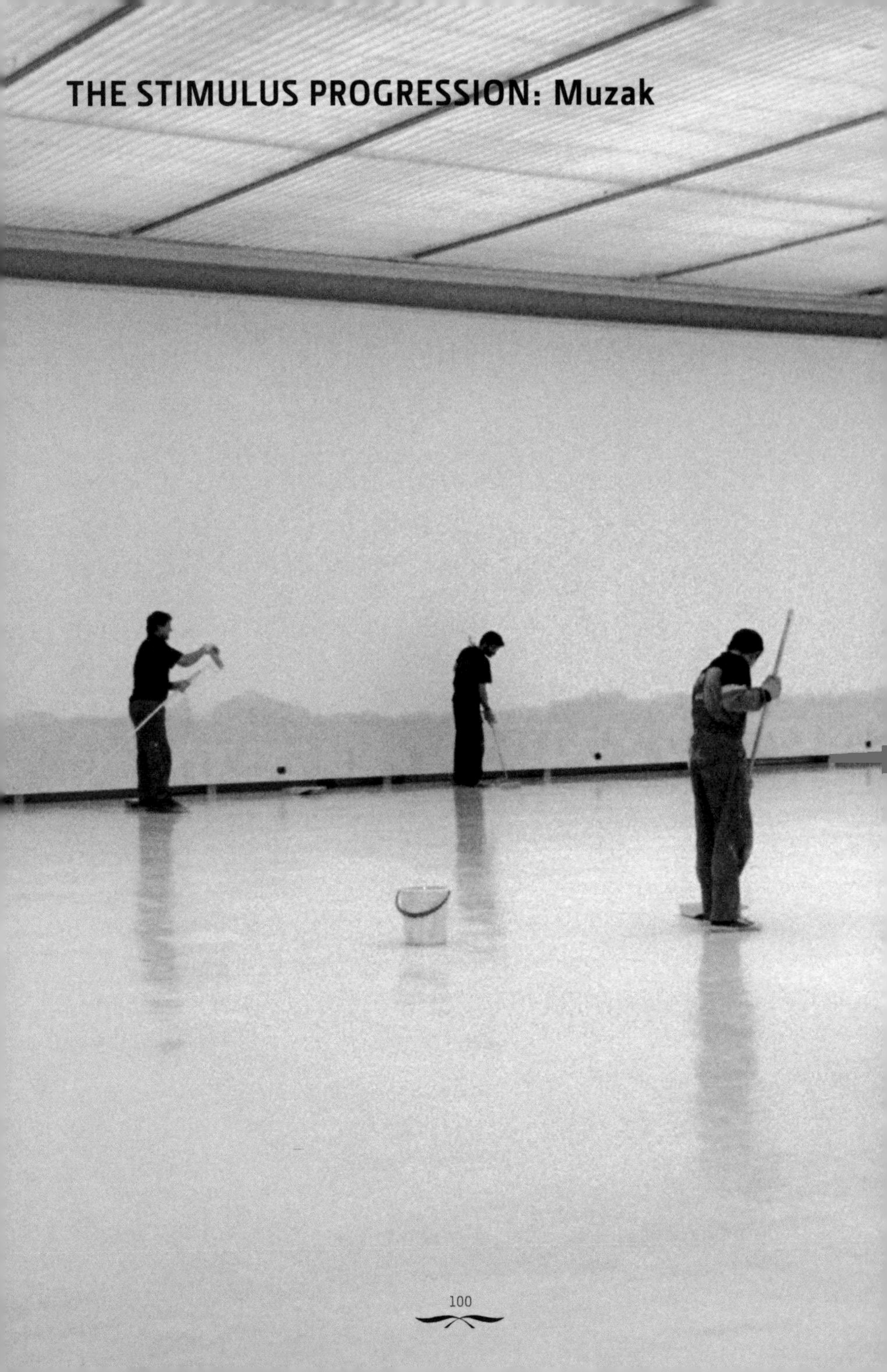

In his *Economic and Philosophical Manuscripts of 1844*, Karl Marx writes, "The forming of the five senses is a labor of the entire history of the world down to the present." The great loser of this history has been aurality. After sight came to the fore in that great visual age, the Enlightenment, aurality's golden age was lost to us forever. That history is silent. Not until Edison's invention of the phonograph in 1877 do we know, with certainty, what sounds our ancestors heard. [1]

In pre-Industrial societies, music ordered the day, providing a continuous conditioning of the environment. Like animals in the wild, individuals sang either individually or in groups. When in groups, singing was always a collective act. Even when one or more particularly talented singers led the tune, everyone in the group contributed to the performance, either as a singer of the narrative, a member of the chorus, or by supporting the rhythm. The rhythm of songs was key to work, coordinating workers' muscles for the repetitive tasks of the day. Songs marked the cyclical time of day and provided the sensation of time passing. Songs commented on the work process, everyday life, or religious themes, thereby establishing a shared bond between co-workers even in the most difficult of situations. Songs sung together at the workplace, at home, and in worship established solid bonds in communities by providing shared experiences and marking the memory of other shared experiences. Music was both a communal activity and, in memorializing events, the beginning of history-writing.

If everyday life was structured by an acoustic rhythm, the repetition of songs was a constant producer of difference. Each time a song was sung, it was original, adapted to the circumstances of the moment. Until the Industrial Revolution, all sounds were unique. Whether they were produced for music, as by-products of human actions, or natural in origin, sounds could not be replicated.

[1] Karl Marx, *Economic and Philosophic Manuscripts of 1844* (New York: International, 1968), 140-141.

The everyday acoustic environment was not, however, a merely temporal activity. It was also spatial, marking out a territory through sound. Music warded off a hostile nature by asserting the presence of humans against the sounds of the wild.

But some sounds could not be tamed. Anthropologists theorize that loud sounds, especially those in the lowest acoustic registers, inspire feelings of awe and dread. Thunder, the ocean, storms, waterfalls, and volcanoes terrified primitive peoples, making them sense that God would soon punish them. Priests and rulers would use church bells, gongs, and the pipe organ to simulate these loud, low-frequency sounds, thereby instilling the sensation that God was present. This sonic God was often not only invisible but also inaudible, produced by infrasonic phenomena. God's infrasonic existence explains why in Judeo-Christian tradition his name is unutterable. Noise, Jacques Attali writes, is capable of disrupting tissues, and carries with it the threat of death. Through harmony, noise can be sublimated. By releasing dissonance, music functions like ritual sacrifice, reproducing the terror of murderous violence, thereby demonstrating how God could redirect destructive forces for mankind's good and, in dissolving the individual in a greater whole, affirms society. [2]

The Industrial Revolution brought radical change to the acoustic landscape of everyday life. Machines on the factory floor produced loud sounds without regard to aesthetics or human comfort. Nor did these new industrial sounds stop at the factory walls: some factories were loud enough to be heard beyond the gates, while trains and later automobiles generated sounds that permeated the city. With machines now the dominant producers of sound, power shifted from the church to capital and the background against which everyday life was lived changed from nature to industry. Workers

[2] Jacques Attali, *Noise: The Political Economy of Music* (Minneapolis: University of Minnesota Press, 1985), 26-31.

had little control over these sounds; they were, in general not participatory, not pleasant, and afforded little variation. Singing was increasingly difficult in this new environment. Industrial machinery created a new rhythm to life. The structure of work in this new situation was also hostile to song. The nineteenth century factory boss and the twentieth century manager replaced the song-leader in the field, but instead of working in concert with their fellows, ordered them around, expecting no response except obedience. In the factory songs of dissatisfaction were not only emotional releases, but could incite revolt as well. Songs commenting on work could not be permitted, and factory owners banned them. Many companies perceived employee-produced music as a distraction from dangerous work with the expensive new machinery. Henry Ford's employees worked in silence. [3]

With capitalism replacing sacred and courtly society, music became autonomous from the sacred. In addition to spreading machine sounds throughout the city, industrialization also allowed the bourgeoisie to amass capital, thereby threatening the cultural exclusivity of the aristocracy. As the newly rich industrialists looked to express their higher cultural standing, they appropriated courtly music for their own entertainment. Music was tied to public architecture and to the metropolis. It is no accident that Garnier's Opéra is the centerpiece of Haussmann's Paris. The musical performance is the center of social life in the City of Light, the place to see and be seen. If the mixing pool of the Opéra's staircase demonstrated a Utopian near-equality—only the Emperor viewed the scene from above—the performance reinforced hierarchy as the seating itself demonstrated social status. The nature of performance changed as well. The rowdy collective audiences of the past were reterritorialized: individuals contemplated the performance in silence, but then united at the end to give their collective verdict through

---

[3] See Mark M. Smith, ed. *Hearing History. A Reader* (Athens: University of Georgia Press, 2004).

applause. At home, the piano took up residence in the bourgeois household. An instrument of unwieldy size and shape and great expense, it verified the owner's status in society. In the city especially only a well-off person could afford to give such space to music.

Thomas Edison developed the first phonograph in 1877, harnessing sound to play it back from a rotating cylinder. The packaging of Edison's cylinders led consumers to call the new medium "canned music," indicating the new status of music as a commodity. A decade later, Emile Berliner invented the gramophone, which played back sound from a revolving disc. Consumers could, for the first time, purchase and control their audio programming as previously only the aristocracy could do. Fans could listen to their favorite songs repeatedly. The weary worker could relax at home and listen to songs on demand, without expending effort.

In *the Recording Angel*, Evan Eisenberg explains that the gramophone and the phonograph objectified music: reducing it to an accompaniment to a piece of furniture and doing away with the need for a public architectural space for enjoyment of music. Instead of listening to music in an opera house, philharmonic hall, church, or pub, from that point on people listened to objects such as record players and radios. Moreover, the development of the mass-produced record made it possible for individuals to collect music as an object, something to admire on a shelf as much as audibly.

The experience of listening to recorded music is a distinct experience from producing music or going to a concert. The ease of playing it back and the lack of a performer allows the listener to perceive the music through distraction, not through active contemplation. Leaving the room or coughing loudly while music is playing from a record is generally not considered rude as it would be in a live performance. Listening to music in one's own home undid the old experience of communal musical appreciation, the mass distribution of a single, recorded piece allowed dispersed

communities to form around a single performance's appreciation regardless of its original time or location.

The appearance of mass-produced music at the turn of the century came at a moment when leisure time was expanding, thereby posing new problems for the recently invented profession of the manager. For if the factory and office demanded new levels of attention from the worker, they also created new heights of monotony. Both the workday and the work-week shortened so that employees could have time to recover from their dull labors, but leisure time had its own dangers: the working class could fall prey either to destabilizing mass-oriented political forces or to drink and unruly individual behavior. Welfare organizations such as the YMCA sprang up to help workers while corporations created organized activities such as sports and adult education. To teach workers lasting values and make the workplace more tolerable, some corporations established programs in which workers either listened to or produced approved music. At Frank Lloyd Wright's Larkin Administration Building in Buffalo, a pipe organ and reproducing piano were installed so that musicians could play for the employees. Henry Ford hired the Detroit Symphony to play for his employees several times a year. Department stores held morning sing-alongs in order to instill politeness in their workers. All this took time out from leisure and allowed a conditioning of the workers' lives. [4]

THE WIRED WIRELESS MASS MEDIUM

The invention of radio at the beginning of the twentieth century further transformed the individual's relationship to the collective by providing a system for instantaneous communication across great distances. During the 1920s, commercial radio broadcasts spread across the air, delivering regular, dependable media experiences that large numbers of individuals could share simultaneously, even while apart. Once purchased, radios assembled these individuals into a mass audience regardless of their literacy or social status, creating the first true mass media. Through the addition of the tuning dial, radio listeners gained the effortless experience of surfing for information across different channels. Listening to the radio was less a private experience enjoyed by an autonomous individual and more a series of individual or small group experiences in which people saw themselves as part of a regionally dispersed body made up of content producers, transmitters, radio signals, receivers, and other listeners whom they never meet personally.

[4] On the emergence of the phonograph see Eisenberg, *The Recording Angel* and Jonathan Sterne, *The Audible Past: Cultural Origins of Sound Reproduction* (Durham: Duke University Press, 2003).

Radio, however, still faced many real limitations: it required large and expensive signal towers; its relatively weak transmissions were easily interrupted by local terrain and would often degrade in poor weather conditions; its signals would drop off due to distance. In 1911, General George Owen Squier, then Chief Signal Officer of the U. S. Army Signal Corps, discovered a solution to these problems, identifying an effective means of audio transmission over electrical power lines using the signal multiplexing he developed to carry multiple channels over one wire. In contrast to wireless radio, transmitting music through the system Squier named "wired wireless" ensured higher signal quality regardless of atmospheric or solar conditions. Weary of the privatization that had marred the early development of the telephone industry, Squier patented his discovery in the name of the American public, making the technology available for free use and development across the nation.

Engineers adapted the new technology to create the first countrywide communications network, allowing the simultaneous delivery of programs through utility lines to remote radio transmitting stations. Squier, however, was not satisfied with the commercial structure of radio, in which programs were funded by intrusive commercials. He envisioned a new network supported by a toll that would make unnecessary the commercials and program interruptions that sponsored, and for Squier, corrupted radio. Squier approached the North American Company, then the nation's largest utility company, to transmit music over their lines. North American responded positively and formed Wired Radio, Incorporated. To avoid problems with broadcast rights to music, North American purchased Breitkopf Publications, Inc., a European music-publishing house, and renamed it Associated Music Publishers.

In 1934, North American formed the Muzak Corporation to transmit music directly to homes in Cleveland. Muzak's name was derived from a merger of the word "music" with "Kodak," a highly technological and reputable company. Squier died later that year, never to see the success of his invention.

Success was not, in any case, immediate. The project in Cleveland fell victim to technological troubles and the development of superheterodyne circuits, vacuum tubes, and volume controls gave radios a technological boost while the ongoing Depression encouraged consumers to stick with a one-time radio purchase over the expense of a long-term lease. For their part, radio companies opposed the idea of Muzak competing for their listeners. In 1938, the Federal Communications Commission severely restricted Muzak's market in radio's favor by forbidding the company from using electrical power lines for broadcast directly into the home. Although Squier's inventions of wired wireless and signal multiplexing would later be widely adopted by cable television broadcasters, Muzak would initially be restricted to commercial venues.

Far from limiting the company, forcing Muzak to target commercial venues instead offered it a clearer mission that would give it an advantage over radio in commercial settings. Recorded music is sold with limited rights of use, generally not including public performance. Licenses for playing recorded media in public were a key source of income for the young record industry, but created new difficulties in tracking the number and locations of its playback. In 1914, the American Society of Composers, Artists, and Publishers (ASCAP) was founded, serving as a member-owned organization to fight for fair compensation when recorded work was publicly performed. The first successful lawsuit pursued by ASCAP, against Shanley's Restaurant in New York City, was heard by the United States Supreme Court. Justice Oliver Wendell Holmes explained his judgment in favor of ASCAP by saying "If music did not pay, it would be given up. Whether it pays or not, the purpose of employing it is profit and that is enough."

By 1920, the administration of music rights had become a major business. While radio stations could license programming for personal performance, they could not track where music was being played and take respon-

sibility for its licensing. The wired wireless subscription service, however, was ideal for this task. Because every Muzak receiver could be uniquely identified, it was easy for Muzak to track who was using their service and what the service was being used for.

Muzak is the perfect commodity. If, as Guy Debord suggests, the spectacle is capital accumulated to the degree that it becomes image, Muzak took this a step further, making visibility a thing of the past.

Muzak reformed in New York City to cater to the hotel and restaurant market, playing in venues like the Chambord, the Stork Club, and the Waldorf Astoria. This time, audio would be sent to clubs through leased telephone lines rather than electric lines. Speakers would be hidden amongst large plants, thereby making the music seem to come out of nowhere and lending it the name "potted palm" music. With the disappearance of any vis-

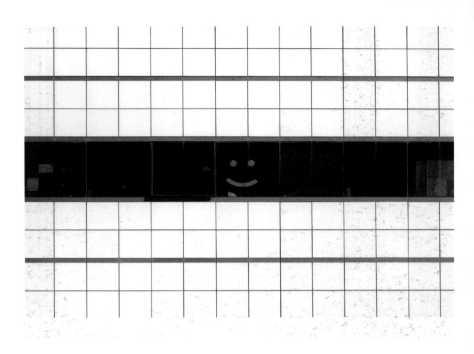

ible means of sound production, Muzak exceeded the gramophone's capacity to make sound autonomous. In delivering programming to the workplace, Muzak soothed the minds of employees, enhancing their productivity while eliminating the distractions caused by commercials, scripted programs, and other verbal content.

Sending music to the workplace was in keeping with the vision that Squier had left for the company. As Chief Signal Officer of the Army Signal Corps, Squier used music to increase the productivity of his secretaries. Afterwards, he investigated ways that music could recapture the benefits of pre-industrial song, in order to soothe the nerves of employees while increasing their output. The idea of using music to improve an environment was not uncommon by the 1930s, when dentists employed music to augment or even replace anesthetic.

Muzak soon proved effective in locations beyond the office or factory floor. As skyscrapers reached ever taller in North American cities, building owners employed Muzak to calm anxious elevator riders, quickly earning its programs the name "elevator music."

New research in the 1930s provided a rationale for Muzak's effects. Named after a study at the Hawthorne Plant of the Western Electric Company in Cicero, Illinois, the Hawthorne Effect explained human relations in the workplace. The study concluded that individuals would be more productive when they knew they were being studied or paid attention to, regardless of the experimental manipulation employed. The workplace, it turned out, was first and foremost a social system made up of interdependent parts. According to this theory, workers would be more influenced by social demands from inside and outside the workplace, by their need for recognition, security, and a sense of belonging, than by the physical environment surrounding them. Being the object of a study made workers feel involved and important. The Hawthorne Effect argued for attention and surveillance instead of architectural or social reforms.

At this time Muzak unreflectively mimicked radio, with a hotel orchestra sound developed by Ben Selvin, a prolific bandleader who had recorded 1,000 records by 1924 and whose Moulin Rouge Orchestra had extensive experience on the air. Named vice-president for recording and programming at the corporation in 1934, Selvin set up Muzak as a radio station, with distinct programs featuring types of music such as marches for breakfast and pipe organs for lunch. Selvin preferred a quiet and restrained sound with few brass instruments and an emphasis on strings. To prevent the music from lulling workers to sleep, Selvin chose popular songs familiar to everyone, thereby keeping workers' attention. Muzak provided a gesture to the workers—deploying the Hawthorne Effect—a constant reminder that the boss was thinking of them.

Within the workplace, Muzak distinguished between four basic conditions—public areas, offices, light industrial settings, and heavy industrial settings—each of which they addressed with a different music program. In industrial settings, where loud noises make traditional background music hard to hear, Muzak turned to sounds with a greater penetration, favoring percussion instruments and melodies with more distinct timbres. Even if the factory was loud, the difference in pitch made the music audible. Studies produced by Muzak showed that it reduced absenteeism in the workplace by 88 per cent.

During the Second World War, the military sponsored scientific research and stimulated management techniques to improve productivity, undertaking extensive research into the playing of music in office and factory environments. These studies, often undertaken by employees of Muzak and its competitors, concluded that silence during repetitive tasks led to boredom while talking was too distracting. Music, on the other hand, did not draw the eye's attention away from work, rather it alleviated fatigue arising from monotonous actions.

The general conclusion of these studies suggested that music affects the body physiologically, stimulating breathing, metabolism, muscular energy, pulse, blood pressure, and internal secretions. This fit neatly with the James-Lange theory developed independently by William James and Carl Lange. The James-Lange theory states that the human nervous system creates automatic changes with regard to experiences in the world. Only once one feels a rise in heart rate, an increase in perspiration, dryness of the mouth, and so on does one experience emotion. By affecting the body physiologically, background music could keep workers' nervous systems calm, thereby giving them greater emotional stability during the difficult days of the war.

Starting during the "Baptism by Fire" of the British during 1940, the BBC's "Music While You Work" program broadcast music made by two live

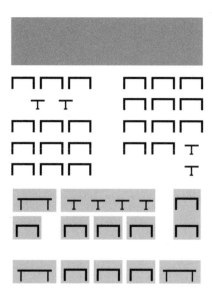

bands to factories to soothe workers returning to work after nights of bombardment, thereby distracting them from dwelling on their predicament. The success was noted in Britain and the United States. Soon after, music was made mandatory for all British war workers. By war's end some 5 million British workers listened to "Music While You Work." By 1943, some 6 million American workers listened to music in the factory.

After the war, corporations continued to be interested in using music to improve productivity. At Muzak, company researchers who had been involved in wartime research came to the conclusion that in addition to the vague increase in productivity that music in the workplace generated through the Hawthorne Effect, the James-Lange theory suggested that music could more deliberately affect the changing attention levels of workers throughout the day to maintain a steady level of productivity.

While Taylorist work practices streamlined industrial manufacturing and office work, they also made these jobs even more monotonous. Without direct supervision, the fatigue and boredom brought about by repetitive tasks could quickly undo the very advances that these new practices hoped to provide. Muzak researchers concluded that varying the tempo of music played to workers throughout the workday was one way of fighting fatigue.

For this they turned to another fundamental observation of modern industrial psychology, the Yerkes-Dodson Law, formulated by Robert M. Yerkes and John D. Dodson in 1908. According to the Yerkes-Dodson Law, optimal performance is attained with a median level of arousal. Too much arousal distracts the worker while too little leads to inertia. The sources of arousal in the office environment can take many forms, and include negative stimuli like stress and anxiety as well as pleasure and comfort or even, as the Hawthorne Effect proved, the act of scientific monitoring itself. The key isn't each moment of arousal itself, but the flow from one moment to the next, and the variation of arousal types. Muzak researchers concluded that since complex work is more engaging, it requires less distraction from background music while simple work, being less arousing, requires more complex music.

Whatever the workplace environment, Muzak set out to maintain a median level of arousal. Researchers observed natural levels of arousal rise and fall throughout the day as well as over fifteen minute cyclical periods. In response, Muzak arranged programs according to a "Stimulus Progression," varying musical energy levels over fifteen-minute segments followed by either thirty-second or fifteen-minute long periods of silence, depending on the subscriber's desire. The length of the Stimulus Progression enhanced productivity by creating distinctly delimited breaks in work activity.

The Stimulus Progression itself was based on Muzak's analysis of its songs for their emotional content and energy levels. Factoring in tempo, type of music, instruments employed, and the size of orchestra, Muzak determined a stimulus value for each song. By the 1950s, Muzak would modulate its level of stimulus during the day to offset decreases in worker efficiency during midmorning and mid-afternoon slumps. The order of the Stimulus Progression was crucial: studies showed that played backwards, it would put listeners to sleep.

The Stimulus Progression was based on the human heartbeat, an average of 72 beats per minute at rest. Playing music faster stimulated listeners, but constantly doing so would make them nervous. Thus, the Stimulus Progression started below 72 bpm, rising during the course of the program. That the Stimulus Progression addressed the heartbeat at rest indicates that Muzak focused not so much on the factory, where workers might exert themselves but on the office, where workers would be sedentary.

Programmed for round-the-clock shifts, Muzak was an endless circadian cycle in which all sounds, including silence, were given space. Eventually, Muzak developed additional programs for use in homes, hospitals, urban environments, government facilities, and outer space. With its omnipresence, Muzak could order our lives temporally. [5]

[5] On the history of Muzak, see Jane Hulting, "Muzak: A Study in Sonic Ideology," (MA thesis, University of Pennsylvania, 1988) and, in particular, Jerri Ann Husch, "Music of the Workplace: A Study of Muzak Culture," (PhD diss., University of Massachusetts, 1984). Stephen H. Barnes, *Muzak, the Hidden Messages in Music: A Social Psychology of Culture,* (Lewiston, NY: E. Mellen Press, 1988) adds little to the Husch work, but is still of interest. Also useful are two popular texts, *Anthony Haden-Guest, The Paradise Program; Travels through Muzak, Hilton, Coca-Cola, Texaco, Walt Disney, and Other World Empires,* (New York,: W. Morrow, 1973) and Joseph Lanza, *Elevator Music: A Surreal History of Muzak, Easy-Listening, and Other Moodsong,* (New York: St. Martin's Press, 1994). There is no room here to discuss Squier's career prior to Muzak, but it is fascinating reading nonetheless. Squier developed military research, multiplexy, and was the second passenger in an airplane. For that see Paul Wilson Clark, Major George Owen Squier: "Military Scientist" (PhD diss., Case Western Reserve University, 1974). Doron K. Antrim, "Music in Industry" *The Musical Quarterly* 29, no. 3 (July 1943), 275-290 provides a first-hand account of the use of music in wartime manufacturing.

'MUZAK FILLS THE DEADLY SILENCES'

Muzak developed during the era of Art Deco architecture and "jazzy" design. Like Art Deco, Muzak was meant to inspire office workers to move along to the increasingly fast pace of the modern corporation. Just as design and architecture evolved from Art Deco to the International Style, Muzak moved to the Stimulus Progression.

The streamlined geometry of Art Deco design attempted to mask the repetitive nature of office work with a representation of the speed and tempo of modern music. But Art Deco failed to keep its promise: fixed in architectural form, it could only represent change, and was not itself capable of changing over time. As workers grew accustomed to Art Deco, they grew bored of it, associating its forms with the overheated exuberance of the 1920s and the desperate salesmanship of the Great Depression. As International Style modern architecture spread in the postwar era, Muzak spread with it. Muzak punctuated activity on the floors of the Johnson Wax Company building, Lever House, the Seagram building, the Chase Manhattan bank building, the Pan Am building, the Sears Tower, the Apollo XI command module and countless other modernist structures. Muzak is the hidden element in every Ezra Stoller photograph of a modernist office interior. By 1950, some 50 million people heard Muzak every year.

Muzak made modernism palatable sonically. The new, hermetically sealed office buildings that the glass curtain wall and postwar air conditioning system permitted were capable of blocking out distracting sounds from outside, but without these sounds, two new conditions emerged. In some areas, office machines, building control systems, and fellow employees became more distracting while in others, you simply had too much quiet making the artificial lack of environmental sound uncomfortably noticeable. Broadcasting Muzak ensured a superior, controlled background condition.

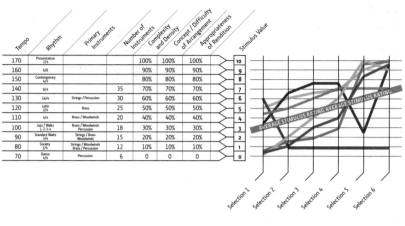

Tempo	Rhythm	Primary Instruments	Number of Instruments	Complexity and Density	Concept / Difficulty of Arrangement	Appropriateness of Rendition	Stimulus Value
170	Presentation 2/4			100%	100%	100%	10
160	6/8			90%	90%	90%	9
150	Contemporary 4/4			80%	80%	80%	8
140	8/4		35	70%	70%	70%	7
130	16/4	Strings / Percussion	30	60%	60%	60%	6
120	Latin 2/4	Brass	25	50%	50%	50%	5
110	4/4	Brass / Woodwinds	20	40%	40%	40%	4
100	Jazz / Waltz 1-2-3-4	Brass / Woodwinds Percussion	18	30%	30%	30%	3
90	Standard Waltz 3/4	Strings / Brass Woodwinds	15	20%	20%	20%	2
80	Society 2/4	Strings / Woodwinds Brass / Percussion	12	10%	10%	10%	1
70	Dance 4/4	Percussion	6	0	0	0	0

Selection 1 · Selection 2 · Selection 3 · Selection 4 · Selection 5 · Selection 6

AVERAGE STIMULUS RATING

Tempo - Number of Prime Accents / Beats Measured by Metronome
Rhythm - Musical Form / Broad Classifications of Popular Music
Predominant Instrumental Useage
Number of Instruments Used in Arrangement
Complexity and Density / Stimulus Through Arrangement Methods
Conceptual Rigor / Nature of Melody and Harmony Combined to Make a Musical Point
Appropriateness of Rendition in Reference to the Original Arrangement

Muzak's slogan during this period was "Muzak fills the deadly silences." But Muzak isn't just invisible to the eyes, in the company's own words, Muzak "is meant to be heard, but not listened to." Aimed at a subliminal level, the immaterial gestures of the Stimulus Progression were neither ornamental nor representational, but rather physiological. Workers did not think about Muzak, they were programmed by it. As soon as Muzak received any requests for songs, they immediately removed them from the library. Like the Fordist worker, Muzak that drew attention to itself was deemed unsuccessful and dismissed.

By filling the deadly silences, Muzak supported modernism and made the impersonality of the Fordist management system more palatable. In bridging melody (individuality) and monotony (the abstract field), Muzak provided an element of accommodation against a background of abstraction, acting as a palliative for both the modern office and for modern architecture. Interactions between individuals that would otherwise have been uncomfortable, such as disciplinary reprimands, terminations, and general office tension could all be alleviated by its soothing background tones.

Composed almost exclusively of love songs stripped of their lyrics, the Stimulus Progression provided a gentle state of erotic arousal throughout the day. Desire, union, and disappointment could all be felt collectively, albeit subconsciously, thereby adding color to the day and blunting the impact of such emotions when real life erupted in the workplace. James Keenen, Ph.D., the Chairman of Muzak's Board of Scientific Advisors concluded that "Muzak promotes the sharing of meaning because it massifies symbolism in which not few but all can participate." Muzak provided the same symbolic experience as pre-industrial song did, but this sharing of meaning happened below the threshold of consciousness.

Whereas in the 1930s Muzak was essentially the same as popular music and radio, by the 1940s it had gone its own way, creating a different level of attention and its own medium. Muzak had pioneered the use of long playing 33 1/3 rpm records in order to create more seamless soundscapes for its functional music. In contrast, RCA Victor's 1949 introduction of the smaller and less expensive 45 rpm disc format allowed popular hits and youth-oriented rock music to be taken almost anywhere and listened to over and over.

Small hand-held personal record players are some of the most important consumer objects of the twentieth century, helping to forge radically new communities among young adults based on consumption and consumer identity, rather than work itself. After a period of economic and technological growth from the first two world wars, a surplus of income allowed teenagers unprecedented freedom from familial restraints and societal mores. Personal record players encouraged listening in private, offering media consumption free from supervision. As the first purely consumer market, youth culture relied heavily on the purchasing and playback of music to express itself and create identity. Young listeners would take apart songs, transcribing lyrics and music and playing the songs themselves. The resulting rock and roll music of the 1950s was the most dramatic singular youth culture movement in history, cutting across class and even chipping away at racial divisions.

But like the prewar modernism of the *avant-garde*, rock and roll was the subject of constant, engaged attention. Muzak, in contrast, corresponded to postwar corporate modernism and was apprehended through distraction. While rock became increasingly abrasive and strove for shock value, Muzak desired not to be heard. Unlike rock, popular with young people but hated by their elders, by the early 1950s Muzak consciously eliminated genres commonly perceived as objectionable.

Theodor W. Adorno may well have outlined the program for postwar Muzak in his 1938 "On the Fetish-Character in Music and the Regression of Listening" when he stated that since contemporary music is "perceived purely as background," it no longer has anything to do with taste: "To like it is almost the same as to recognize it." In a world of completely identical choices, recognition itself has become impossible. Preference, Adorno suggests, "depends merely on biographical details or on the situation in which things are heard." Adorno contends that active listening is at odds with contemporary music as it would reveal the banality of its arrangement. Instead, of attention, Adorno suggests, contemporary music is based on mindless repetition of certain material and performers. [6]

[6] Theodor A. Adorno, "On the Fetish-Character in Music and the Regression of Listening," *Essays on Music* (Berkeley: University of California Press, 2002), 288-317.

Like air-conditioning and fluorescent lighting, Muzak flourished as an acclimatization technology for the extreme environment of the skyscraper. Soon, however, it undid its host structure. Muzak made vast, horizontal interior spaces, previously usable only for warehouses, habitable by covering up the noise that would build up in large floorplates. The lower costs of building these new, flat structures in less expensive suburban locations and the growing efficiency of the same data communication technologies that Muzak itself employed soon made tall buildings obsolete.

The development of cybernetic theories after the war transformed management structures and made the office floor a source for innovation and positive change. Having learned from the Hawthorne Effect, managers no longer acted as overseers trying to keep employees from wasting time and becoming distracted from their tasks and instead encouraged employees to take on greater responsibility for themselves and their own positions within the corporation. In order for employees to share information and expertise, social interaction became crucial and open environments replaced closed offices and executive floors. Large interiors facilitated greater freedom of com-

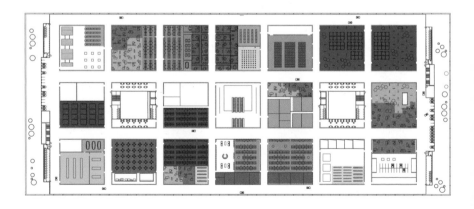

munication. In particular, the open plans and horizontal methods of organization developed by proponents of Büro Landschaft became a major aspect of both late modern architecture and management strategy.

Open plans eliminated walls completely or replaced them with partitions to allow for greater flexibility in programme and increased interaction among employees. This openness, however, also enables the unimpeded circulation of unpleasant background noise as well, including the distracting sounds of office machines, ventilation systems, coworkers, and exterior traffic. Muzak masked these background sounds, helping employees and customers focus on messages and sounds that matter while adding a layer of sensory engagement to an otherwise blank architecture.

The horizontality of the open plan is the very basis of contemporary society. It enables fluid structures that can more effectively respond to changing situations. In this condition, Muzak's ability to structure an environment invisibly offers a model for control. In his "Postscript on the Societies of Control," Gilles Deleuze traces the transition from a society of discipline to a society of control. As both Bataille and Foucault point out, architecture was the instrument for discipline and order throughout the eighteenth and nineteenth centuries. Devices for creating enclosure and allowing for the supervision of many workers by a few managers, buildings structured society. By the middle of the twentieth century, however, this model no longer held power. In place of the 'molds' made by enclosures, Deleuze suggests that we are dominated by subtle modulations. No longer driven by fear, work is now based on identifying with, and entering, the flow. The Stimulus Progression ensured the success of modulation in the workplace. [7]

[7] Deleuze, "Postscript on the Societies of Control," 3-7.

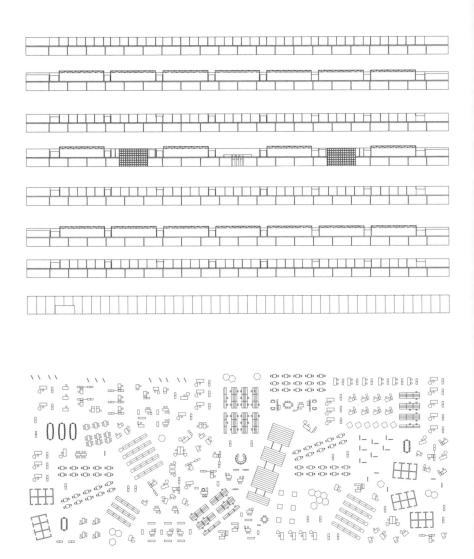

Muzak now faces individuals with a changed sensorium. The constant flow of changes across society has made us less responsive to any particular change. Over time, our sensorium has grown more able to tolerate the shock of the new. Once shocking, both skyscrapers and sprawl have become everyday. This condition is also evidenced by changes in our relationship to music. While Elvis was radical in the 1950s, he is background today. The speed by which we assimilate newness in musical culture has increased greatly over the last twenty years. Played over and over, "God Save the Queen" and "Like A Virgin" have become tunes we hum along with absent-mindedly, their radical message sublimated. These popular hits work the same way that Muzak's earlier instrumentals did, acting as a stimulating but blank texture within the empty spaces of work and consumption.

When present, emotion becomes sublimated into affect that can be turned on and off at will. Violently rejecting the hippie ethic of free love and peace to the world, Punk rock was the last musical or cultural movement that presented an alternative emotion. By the late 1970s, New Wave had finished with emotion altogether, partly because new amplification technology made it no longer necessary as a means of reaching audiences (it is no accident that the Cars were the loudest band of their day). Thus John Lennon's 1970 *Plastic Ono Band* was a raw wound, informed by Arthur Yanov's Primal Scream Therapy in its quest to break through the veneer of rationalism that Fordism created through the aural expression of accumulated pain. In contrast, Tears for Fears' 1983 *the Hurting* addressed the same theme via the inflectionless lines of a synthepop dance song: "Shout, shout/Let it all out/These are the things I can do without/Come on/I'm talking to you/So come on." Ten years later, the commercial acceptance of Kurt Cobain points out how today all resistance, sadness, and pain can be experienced as affect. With Nirvana, alienation was no longer a matter of struggle but rather could be accepted as a mood or intensity. Even prior to Cobain's death in 1994, Muzak, which was based in

Seattle during the decade of the "Seattle Sound," had created an instrumental version of "Smells Like Teen Spirit." Cobain's inheritance, "Emo Rock," reduces emotion to a genre. No longer does music have to be as inflectionless as New Wave. Now it can mime emotion, comforting us with the knowledge that it is just a mood to plug in and out of at will throughout the course of our day.

Always ahead of the curve, Muzak abandoned the Stimulus Progression in favor of "Audio Architecture" in the 1980s. At this point, the amount of stimulation received in the daily environment far exceeded any ability of the engineers at Muzak to modulate such forces. Overstimulated, individuals can no longer be affected by increases in data alone. In response, Muzak's programmers don't style themselves as engineers or scientists. Instead they harness this excess of data to become "Audio Architects," a term that indicates that they construct environments, and that Muzak is as much art as science.

The sensorial overload of contemporary culture means that even original songs are no longer distracting. Today most of Muzak's channels broadcast originals, not reorchestrated versions. The result is that Muzak's audio programming has become even more invisible: if the music is audible, its source is no longer discernible.

The culture industries have made it possible for even the most wild and subversive content to be consumed by everyone. With repeated airplay, song lyrics lose their meaning, turning all music into a background of moods without emotional depth. Today, in a radically segmented demographic market, Muzak's customers can choose from a variety of programs that include all forms of music, picking the channels and moods most appropriate to their audience's needs and can request custom selections designed to enhance their unique brand personality.

For the post-Fordist marketplace, Muzak addresses its audience's emotions, creating moods rather than seeking to manipulate attention. Muzak employs the technique of "Atmospherics" to create a distinct ambient audio environment for a particular retail environment. Through a careful choice of music, together with appropriate selections of colors, furniture, and accessories, a store can conjure the image of an entire lifestyle.

Inside a store, Muzak's cozy, ordered atmospherics offer a contrast to the chaos outside and stimulate the consumer's desire to purchase. Disoriented by noise, the proliferation of signs, and the emptiness and hustle that occurs within the vastness of either the mall or the contemporary city, the individual enters a store seeking solace and emotional comfort within a clearly ordered set of goods and experiences.

Atmospherics also solve an earlier problem that Muzak faced in stores and restaurants. Directed at transient occupants of a space, the old public area Muzak channel had a shorter programming cycle, thereby irritating workers who had to be in the space for the entire day and felt relentlessly sped up. In contrast, Atmospherics aim at a culture that unites workers and shoppers in a total community. Within the workplace, Muzak not only helps stimulate employees so that they produce more, Atmospherics form a corporate culture that supports group hegemony and shared cultural references among radically different individuals. With Muzak, the ultimate product of the retail or corporate space becomes consumers and workers themselves.

The transition from the Stimulus Progression to Atmospherics echoes the shift from Fordism to post-Fordism. The Stimulus Progression was a manifestation of the Fordist plan: it was temporal, linear, and directed at the individual, who would use it to fine-tune his or her own self. The Stimulus Progression was primarily, although not exclusively, about production. In contrast, Atmospherics are spatial, nonlinear, and self-contained. Atmospherics replace the Stimulus Progression with Quantum Modulation, which does not vary in intensity or mood. On the contrary, under Quantum Modulation, songs are numerically indexed according to criteria such as tempo, color (light or dark) rhythm, popularity and so on to ensure that the same intensity can be maintained even as the music appears to have changed. Atmospherics address individuals as they traverse different ambiances throughout their everyday lives. Unlike the relatively simple goals of the Stimulus Progression, Atmospherics propose that work is a form of consumption and that consumption is a form of work. [8]

[8] More information on the recent history of Muzak can be found in Jonathan Sterne, "Sounds Like the Mall of America: Programmed Music and the Architectonics of Commercial Space," *Ethnomusicology* 41, no. 1 (Winter, 1997): 22-50, as well as in David Owen, "The Soundtrack of Your Life: Muzak in the Realm of Retail Theater," *New Yorker*, April 10, 2006, 66-71 and on the corporation's Web site, http://www.muzak.com.

THE HUMAN CHAMELEON

Fordist modernism understood that inserting the individual into a larger, overarching plan—be it for a city or a corporation—would appear to give a logical rationale to the process of mass industrialization while providing a theological relief from the uncertainties of modernity, creating a sort of Hawthorne Effect in the public realm. If initially the plan forced individuals to look inward and discipline themselves, the need for constant adjustment and better guidance led Fordist modernism to more explicitly guide individuals from outside. Through the Stimulus Progression, Muzak was an early form of such human programming. Turning to the background condition instead of plans is a more contemporary approach that does away with the need to guide individuals directly.

For the contemporary world, the plan, which addresses the individual as an individual, is too direct. We do not mean to suggest that Althusser's idea that ideology interpellates the individual was wrong, only that individuals are increasingly dissolving and that interpellation is the last thing that power needs. On the contrary, both plan and ideology are obsolete. The background condition eschews any form of top-down control. Background conditions are passively effective, they simply offer individuals the seductive freedom to join in and become a part of something greater instead of actively demanding allegiance.

In "Mimicry and Legendary Psychasthenia," Roger Caillois observes how the process of mimicry amongst animals and insects is not so much a defensive measure as an overwhelming drive. The Phyllia, for example, looks like a leaf so much that it is prone to eating its own kind. But mimicry is not necessary for many insects, who have other defenses or are inedible. Instead, Caillois observes an "instinct of renunciation" that leads creatures to a reduced form of existence in which they lose their distinction from the world and give up consciousness and feeling. Caillois concludes that in our world space is far more complex: the subject is undermined within these spaces from the start. [9]

With the Stimulus Progression abandoned for Atmospherics, and the plan replaced by the background, the individual becomes a human chameleon, lacking either strong sense of self or a guiding plan, but instead constantly looking outward for social cues, seeking an appropriate background condition to settle upon so as to comfortably lose distinction from the world.

Today, difference itself has attained its own level of banality and acceptance. Ever since Marlo Thomas and Steve Jobs, the media machine ritualistically admonishes us to "Be Yourself" and "Think Different" to the point that we cannot understand what is genuine difference and what is contrived for

[9] Roger Callois, "Mimicry and Legendary Psychasthenia" *October* 31 (Winter, 1984): 16-32.

the sake of appearance. Such difference for its own sake is akin to Internet porn: an endless proliferation of images, each meant to arouse and titillate more than the others. Although in the early twentieth century the individual still feared reification, or being turned into a thing by the Fordist system, the human chameleon finds that identifying with the system of objects or images is easy. The human chameleon seeks cues from things as well as from other beings. If not a Mies chair or Karim Rashid, then perhaps something from Pier 1 imports or Pottery Barn will do.

Unable to find progress or direction, the human chameleon follows Freud's Pleasure Principle, seeking to blend in to its surroundings but, when that gets to be too much, breaks with them and seeks out a new environment to identify with. This can happen at various scales. We can choose our citizenship, our religion, our career, our sexual practices, even our gender. We can identify with our diverse friends, family members, ad models, television actors, serial killers, porn stars, cartoon characters such as Dilbert, and Internet avatars at will. We find pleasure in the process of identification as we see others with the same desires we have. We are less and less distinct individuals and more and more surfers on a wave of mass subjectivities held by many people all at once. In order to function within the contemporary city, we have all become human chameleons without a sense of home. Beyond merely moving from place to place, we move from self to self according to the social conditions we find ourselves in.

As the most visible products of society that literally shaped our environment, buildings have always provided social cues. Architecture creates group relationships by articulating moods and milieus within the ubiquitous horizontality of the contemporary urban realm. In the continuous construction of posturbanity, architecture now takes on the same role that Muzak played within the office block. It adds color to our lives. Sometimes it is fast, sometimes it is slow. On rare, special occasions, it is engaging, more often it is banal and background. Architectural gestures that signal "individuality," such as those of Art Deco, postmodernism, or deconstructivism require difference or shock-value in order to be effective. None of these gestures can be sustained indefinitely. Instead, individual works of architecture now become examples of Atmospherics: a relationship between emotional forms whereby a sense of movement, from effect to effect, is generated for the multitude to experience. Stimulus Progression is replaced by Quantum Modulation. We no longer change to create growth and make progress, but to make one day progress differently than the others. The variation of stimuli within the built environment helps us to remain engaged with the world by adjusting to constant change.

Architecture first fully realizes its potential with the mirror glass curtain wall building, developed in the 1970s. The reflections of the structure's surroundings in the surface create a façade of infinite variation while the disappearance of clearly defined window openings replaces the bourgeois notion of the individual with a limitless free space organized solely by a grid. Transparency is replaced not with opacity but with the perpetual flux of the world itself.

Just as Muzak ordered the background condition of the late modern office building, it now makes possible the contemporary condition in which the city becomes a background condition, rendering the delirious vertical expressiveness of the skyscraper obsolete. Today contemporary culture can absorb any content while posturbanity can absorb any amount of difference. Just as the horizontal office building made obsolete the skyscraper, new telecommunications technology—cell phones, email, and instant messaging—undid the need for the horizontal world of office landscape. Physical boundaries no longer impede communication and open space no longer enables it.

Instead, office plans merely become infill, endlessly adapting to real estate footprints. Previously a marker of difference and visibility, architecture is now a background condition. But architecture does not merely go away, it is transformed. Every gesture and emotion produced through architectural form becomes a variation along a Stimulus Progression deployed throughout the city. Minimalism, the Blob, and the Spanish Revival seamlessly coexist in the city without qualities.

In the absence of real public spaces and collective icons, empty visual markers are developed to signify the presence of culture within a city. A tacit agreement has been reached between developers and urban planners: cutting edge concert halls and museums, McMansions, historic districts, and limitless sprawl co-exist merrily in the contemporary city. [10] This urban condition makes possible the necessary illusion that individuation and autonomy remain options even as society continues to move toward immaterial culture.

In 1977 Jacques Attali wrote: "No organizing society can exist without structuring differences at its core. No market economy can develop without erasing those differences in mass-production. The self-destruction of capitalism lies in this contradiction, in the fact that music leads a deafening life: an instrument of differentiation, it has become a locus of repetition." [11] Twenty years later, we are deep in the "crisis of proliferation" he predicted. As the lessons of industrial psychology and Muzak suggest, even meaningless change and variation make us feel like someone or something is responding to us, filling the deadly silence of the city with a form of simulated interaction. Likewise, contemporary architecture creates a catalogue of prefigured affective conditions that allow for variation while accepting that mass difference is a fundamental requirement for living with total universalization. Deleuze's idea of difference in repetition now becomes the prime operating principle for capital. [12]

[10] Kazys Varnelis, "Cathedrals of the Culture Industry," *Forum Annual*, November 2004, 35-40.

[11] Attali, 5.

[12] Gilles Deleuze, *Difference and Repetition*, (New York: Columbia University Press, 1994).

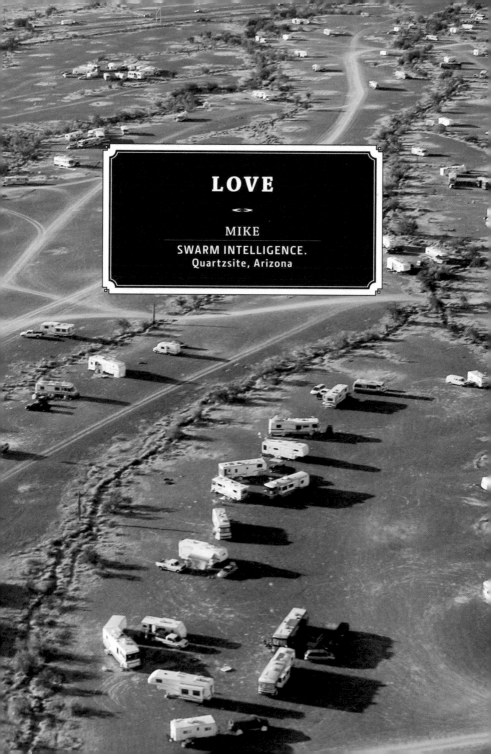

LOVE

◆

MIKE

SWARM INTELLIGENCE.
Quartzsite, Arizona

MIKE

On the tenth of September 1945 in Fruita, Colorado, farmer Lloyd Olsen's
wife Clara asked him to slaughter a chicken so she could make a special dinner
for her mother-in-law. Olsen chose a plump five and a half month old
Wyandotte rooster and chopped off its head with an ax. While freshly killed
chickens normally survive a few seconds or even minutes before dying, this
chicken showed no signs of having been adversely impacted by his decapi-
tation and soon rejoined his chicken friends, pecking at the ground as if he
still had a beak. The next morning, Olsen found the chicken still alive and,
profoundly moved by the chicken's devotion to life, decided to spare it.

Olsen named the chicken Mike and began feeding him grain by hand, giving him water to drink through an eyedropper and dropping little bits of gravel
down Mike's esophagus to help him digest the grain in his gullet. Treated generously, Mike grew from two and a half to eight pounds in eighteen months of
headless life. A post-mortem examination later proved that Mike's staying power was the result of the farmer botching the execution by landing his ax a bit
too high and leaving Mike with just enough brain stem to continue functioning.

Farmer Olsen recognized that Mike's refusal to die was unique and that
others would find in him the inspiration and joy that he had. With the encour-
agement of a promoter named Hope Wade, he set out on a national tour
showing "Miracle Mike, the Headless Wonder Chicken," to curiosity seekers
willing to pay up to twenty-five cents for the experience of seeing Mike,

together with a pickled chicken head in a jar. The head, however, was not Mike's, which the Olsen's cat had eaten, but another chicken's. Soon Farmer Olsen was making $4,500 a month from Mike, a princely sum. Other farmers became jealous and attempted to botch executions on their own roosters to get a piece of the action. Although one rooster, Lucky, lived eleven days without a head, none could challenge Mike's longevity.

But Farmer Olsen's relationship with Mike was one of love, not mere exploitation; he was drawn to Mike's perseverance, his will to live, and his kinship with Mike. Mike was merely a thing, as his execution by the farmer affirms bluntly. With the failure of the act, however, the farmer recognized his own thing-like nature, his similarity to Mike, and dedicated himself to keeping the chicken alive. Tragically, while on tour and staying in a motel in the Arizona desert, the friendship of headless chicken and man came to an end. Mike began to choke and after Olsen was unable to find the dropper he used to clear the chicken's esophagus, his friend Mike died. [1]

During his lifetime, the headless chicken proved a tremendous success with the public because he was cute. As Daniel Harris observes in *Cute, Quaint, Hungry, and Romantic*, cuteness is never the result of aesthetic perfection. On the contrary, it is linked to the grotesque, the malformed, and the damaged. Like Mike, stuffed animals are cute because they lack appendages to attack us with. Although most stuffed animals usually do not lose their

---

[1] Steve Silverman, *Einstein's Refrigerator: And Other Stories from the Flip Side of History* (Kansas City, MO: Andrew McNeel, 2001), 3-6.

heads—Ugly Dolls being a notable exception—they do invariably suffer from some form of damage that cripples them, thereby taming them and making them harmless and dependent on us. Most teddy bears have been aggressively declawed by having their paws—and often even their forearms—removed. Many stuffed animals have had their mouths sewn shut altogether, still others have had their teeth extracted or transformed from hard incisors to floppy bits of felt. Our desire to create pitiable—and therefore lovable—creatures is so great that we insist on reshaping living creatures as well, creating freakish genetically altered pets such as the tiny, short-lived Chihuahua, the tailless Manx cat or the Tennessee Fainting Goat, a bug-eyed ruminant bred to possess myatonia, a genetic heart condition that forces it to drop, immobile, to the ground when startled. Naturally, fainting goats are more frequently and deliberately startled than any other breed of goat. Like Mike, these maimed creatures cannot defend themselves or exist on their own and inspire pity, making us desire to hug and hold them. [2]

In addition to his being cute, Mike also exemplifies our complicated relationship with animals and things. This is made clear by Georges Bataille in his 1948 book, *Theory of Religion*, written only a few short years after Mike's death. The animal, Bataille explains, lives in immanence, a religious and philosophical state where being and spirit exist entirely at one with and within the world. Thus, when one animal eats another, the eater does not affirm its difference

[2] Daniel Harris, "Cute" in *Cute, Quaint, Hungry and Romantic* (New York: Da Capo Press, 2001), 1-22.

from the eaten. Even if one animal has proved itself more powerful than the other, Bataille writes, there is "never anything between them except that quantitative difference. The lion is not the king of the beasts: in the movement of the waters he is only a higher wave overturning the other, weaker ones." For men, however, there is nothing more foreign than this state of animality. We cannot imagine immanence, Bataille explains. Our world is literally constituted by our difference from it, by the fact that we imagine ourselves not as objects but as subjects. If, as in Zen Buddhism, we contemplate being One with the world, we do so with the full knowledge that we are not One with it. This arises, Bataille explains, because we produce tools and plan for the future. In contrast, animals exist only at the level of consumption, at the moment. When we actively think of production, however, we anticipate the future and that tears us out of the plane of immanence. As a consequence, we begin to perceive the world—animal, thing, tool, other beings, even other people—as objects.

The animal, Bataille writes, "has lost its status as man's fellow creature..." An animal no longer exists for itself, but also in order that it may be domesticated or killed. Roasted, grilled, boiled, cut into sushi, fricasseed, or poached, the animal becomes a thing. Unlike the first men, we do not merely eat animals, we transform them and prepare them prior to ingestion. With garnish, sauces, condiments, and spices we turn them into sensuous and aesthetic objects, and, in doing so, affirm that they are objects from the start. Our own bodies are different, posing problems for us when we die. Flesh confirms our animal-like nature, but unlike animals, we are also filled with spirit, and are therefore capable of transcending to the divine realm. Thus, when a human dies, instead of eating the body, we revere it, treating it as more god-like than ever, the emptiness of the corpse being an affirmation of spirit. This fact, Bataille explains, is why ancient cultures built pyramids and spent so much time on mummies. The spirit's departure from the corpse and the ritual put into its passing, proves that, at the very least, man is not animal. [3]

As with Hegel's master-slave dialectic, however, to subordinate is to alter oneself. By subjugating nature, Bataille explains, we tie ourselves to a subjugated nature. Bataille suggests that in producing food for others, the farmer himself runs the danger of losing his identity by being confused with the process of food production itself. This is why, Bataille continues, ancient man would sacrifice the first fruits of the harvest or a head of livestock. The destruction proves that we do not depend on the victim. The act of "unintelligible caprice" destroys the utility aspect of the victim, who would be killed anyway, but instead of being put to productive ends is wasted. Sacrifice undoes the relation of dependence and, as a consequence, the sacrificer turns the victim into part of the divine world, thereby bringing it into the human realm, which is suffused with the divine. Perversely, in making the killing utterly wanton, the sacrifice redresses the wrong of killing the animal. Sacrifice restores the animal to a world of spirit from which we tore it by making it useful in the first place. [4]

[3] Georges Bataille, *Theory of Religion* (New York: Zone Books, 1989), 39.

[4] Bataille, 49.

Sacrifices, Bataille points out, are made at festivals, sites of unfettered consumption where the arts come together to momentarily undo any possibility of production and simulate the lost state of immanence. But the bacchanalian nature of festival exists only within defined limits and the blurring of distance is merely temporary. As society developed, the sacrifice itself was codified, replaced by symbolic things with merely ritual meaning. For a time, as the West expanded to dominate the globe, its need for expansion ensured that production of these goods would still be subordinated to a greater military whole. But by the time Western society had reached the limits of the Earth, production had already become a thing in itself, directed toward the material betterment of human life. This, Bataille posits, initiated the reign of autonomous things, the world of industry. Seeing the world solely in terms of production and, unable to rise above it, humanity became thing-like as well, leading Georg Lukács to observe and describe the phenomenon of humans and human relations becoming "reified." [5]

But Bataille writes, the world of production was too successful. Already in his day, during the brief hours in which Mike walked the Earth, Bataille sensed that production had reached the point of excess beyond which it could not go. In its stead rises a world dominated by consumption, excess, and waste. Today, production has fled the developed world and is strangling the planet with its wild proliferation of meaningless objects. As Jean Baudril-

[5] Bataille, 92-94. Georg Lukács, *History of Class Consciousness* (London: Merlin Press, 1971), 224.

lard observes, at the differing scales of our bodies, national economies, and the world, "Lack isn't the real problem, it is surplus. And surplus, as you know, you can't get rid of it." [6] The world is filled with the obese. This pathological excess of obesity, a proliferation of bodily flesh and a ceaseless proliferation of objects, Baudrillard concludes, is more than anything, a form of disappearance. Consumption becomes an end in itself, detrimental to life instead of sustaining it, erasing all possible meaning in the world around us. [7]

What next, then? There are signs suggesting that the order of things is finally emerging from its long silence. The International Telecommunication Union predicts that soon the biggest users of the Internet will be things. Objects will report about themselves, but also speak to each other. We will report to the objects as they become ever more sentient. [8] Evidence of this can be seen in the child's toy Furby which, like Mike, has no head and needs feeding and love in order to grow. Our dream has always been to return to the state of immanence, the world of things that we lost so long ago. Soon we may be able to do so, not by reducing ourselves, but by giving ourselves up to serving the world of objects in perpetuity.

[6] Jean Baudrillard, *The Conspiracy of Art* (New York: SEMIOTEXT(E), 2005), 84-85.

[7] Jean Baudrillard, *The Revenge of the Crystal* (London: Pluto Press, 1999), 165-166.

[8] International Telecommunication Union, *The Internet of Things* (Geneva: International Telecommunication Union, 2005).

In *Empire*, Michael Hardt and Antonio Negri describe how the withering of the nation-state and the rise of immaterial labor produce a new form of imperial sovereignty, a network power so complete and total that it lacks any exterior. For their landmark sequel, *Multitude*, they identify a counter-force arising within Empire, a networked swarm that communicates and self-organizes without losing its sense of difference or developing into hierarchical forms of rule. The "multitude," as they call it, has no center or readily identifiable organization, but is by no means anarchic, possessing a swarm intelligence much as groups of insects or birds do.

Multitude is the product of a transformation in industrial production from the fixed structures and hierarchies of Fordism to the flexible structures and distributed networks of late capitalism. Hardt and Negri suggest that unlike the Fordist mass, which is defined by sameness, the multitude never ceases to lose its inherent difference. Each agent understands itself not as part of the mass, but as an individual cooperating with others through centerless networks. Against the dictatorship of Empire, Hardt and Negri believe the multitude can achieve immanence and, in so doing, find the means to self-govern and self-organize.

Hardt and Negri's notion of swarm intelligence is indebted to the new science of emergent systems which proposes to explain how a large number of independent agents, each subscribing to simple rules, can produce complex structures such as the stock market, cells in a body, ant colonies, fractal geometries, cities, beehives, or open source software. As each agent interacts with others, common goals emerge and larger structures form, many of which are well beyond the ability of each individual agent to understand.

Unlike a grouping of insects or geometric structures, the multitude is composed of individuals who can use technologies to communicate. To be sure, as Hardt and Negri point out, the multitude is made possible by contemporary technologies of communications. Telecommunications technologies allow us to maintain close relationships with friends who have moved far away as well as with individuals we have never met face-to-face. No longer tied to others unlike ourselves but in close physical proximity, we can easily establish and maintain ties that cross physical and territorial boundaries, carrying on conversations with isolated individuals both near and far. [1]

This does not mean that face-to-face interaction is obsolete. On the contrary, as geographer Ronald F. Abler writes in his seminal article for Bell Telephone Magazine, "What Makes Cities Important," "the production, exchange and distribution of information is critical to the function of the modern metropolis...cities are communications systems." [2] Unlike the city of old, which produced the homogeneous citizen out of disparate immigrants, the contemporary city leads individuals to cultivate difference. But difference can't be cultivated in isolation. To feel authentic, difference must emerge with the support of others who share in that difference. The result is a proliferation of clusters, groups of people cultivating the same differences and eccentricities, generally existing in discrete, localized spaces but bound together by global networks. In turn, these clusters are made up of overlapping microcommunities, groups dedicated to specific activities and often extreme lifestyles such as Star Trek fandom, Lacanian psychoanalysis, machinima production, Kundalini yoga of the 3HO school, modern architecture, the Lifestyle, No Limit Texas Hold'Em Poker, or bird watching. Dense urban areas offer the possibility for individuals to meet others in such micro-communities. [3]

1 Michael Hardt and Antonio Negri, *Multitude: War and Democracy in the Age of Empire* (New York: Penguin Press, 2004).

2 Ronald Abler, "What Makes Cities Important," *Bell Telephone Magazine* March-April 1970, 15.

3 Michael J. Weiss, *The Clustered World: How We Live, What We Buy, and What it All Means About Who We Are* (New York: Little, Brown, and Company, 1999) and Steven Johnson, "Friends 2005: Hooking Up," *Discover*, September 2005, 22.

But this is the posturban era and just as there is no exterior to Empire, so too there is no place left outside the urban condition. If the 1950s and 1960s were the great decades of suburban growth, when inhabitants in both the United States and Europe fled the city for the suburbs, the last decade has been marked by the rapid expansion of the exurban realm. As suburbs have themselves been colonized by cafés, alternative music stores, and art museums, the city has been invaded by shopping malls as well as big box stores such as Home Depot. Rural ways of life have, at long last, vanished. Agriculture has either become thoroughly industrialized or a boutique industry, doctorate-holding farmers hand-pressing extra virgin olive oil or hand-rubbing Waygu cattle to create an Arcadia without hunger or toil, a peasant world that never existed. With the rural gone, exurbia is free to recolonize the land, taking a working landscape and making it a landscape of visual consumption.

Exurbia undoes the traditional familial ties of people to the land, replacing them with a new kind of homogeneity based on the urban phenomena of clustering and micro-communities. For those people so tied to their lifestyles and micro-communities that they identify thoroughly with them, exurbia offers Utopia. Neo-hippies, land speed record fanatics, Klansmen, millionaire skiers, back-country snowboarders, organic cattle ranchers, yachters, recluse billionaires, golfers, dirt bikers, woodworkers, amateur gold miners, and sex addicts all can find exurban communities to suit their lifestyle and live out their fantasies.

If the city is characterized by cultivated diversity, exurbia accommodates clusters seeking voluntary homogeneity. Exurbanites generally avoid situations in which they encounter individuals unlike themselves. In exurbia, group identity is formed by a collective sameness rather than group interaction and communication. To be clear, however, exurbanites often only want to immerse themselves temporarily. Exurbia is the realm of

the retirement home, the second home, the time-share, and the bed and breakfast. Exurbia is a stopover to dwell in for a few days, a few weeks, or a few decades. Nor is exurbia isolated. Just like everywhere else, exurban areas are networked together, forming virtual clusters of similar communities throughout the world.

But as exurban areas develop over time, their insular nature allows for a new kind of diversity. Adjacent neighborhoods develop and coexist which are radically different, creating almost self-contained worlds where interaction is hardly necessary or likely among neighbors. [4]

In search of an urban form for the multitude, an emergent urbanism, we turn to exurbia. For even as much has been made of medieval towns and villages as examples of emergence, these are far from our present-day reality and the medieval villagers are far from the multitude.

[4] David Brooks, "Take a Ride to Exurbia," *The New York Times*, November 9, 2004, Section A, 23.

THE CAPITAL FOR THE MULTITUDE

If there were a capital for the multitude—and by definition there can be no such thing—it would be Quartzsite, Arizona. During the scorching desert summer, Quartzsite is a sleepy town of 3,397 inhabitants, but every year between October and March, a new breed of nomad descends upon the town as hundreds of thousands of campers bring their motorhomes to Quartzsite. These "snowbirds," generally retirees from colder climates, settle in one of the more than seventy motorhome parks in the area or in the outlying desert administered by the Bureau of Land Management (BLM).

The BLM and local law enforcement agencies estimate that a total of 1.5 million people—some recent reports suggest in excess of 2 million—spend time in the Quartzsite area between October and March, a mass migration that temporarily forms one of the fifteen largest cities in the United States. If all of these residents inhabited Quartzsite at once, the result would be a more populous urbanized area than Dallas, San Jose, or San Diego, possibly even bigger than Phoenix or Philadelphia, America's fifth largest city.

Quartzsite is the id for Los Angeles and all generic, horizontal cities of the contemporary era. These "urban sprawl" cities, such as Phoenix, Dallas, and Houston are products of mobility, transitory architecture, and relatively little planning. And yet even though architects and planners hate such cities, these kind of communities remain popular with people.

But if Quartzsite is sprawl, it is super-dense sprawl. Quartzsite makes a radical break with the surrounding emptiness. Although it rejects vertical density and permanence, Quartzsite achieves a remarkable horizontal density as motorhome is parked next to motorhome. Even the largest class of motorhomes is hardly more than 30 square meters in size. With motorhome parked next to motorhome, often to access common infrastructure such as water or power, the 94.0 square kilometers of Quartzite are filled with campers. With the majority of Quartzsite's campgrounds within town boundaries, a rough estimate—assuming 1 million inhabitants at its peak—would suggest that Quartzsite has some 10,000 inhabitants per square kilometer, roughly the same as the density of New York City. Since statistics at Quartzsite are hard to come by, even if we conservatively halved that number or, even more cautiously, quartered it, Quartzsite would be far denser than Atlanta with its 1,121 residents per square kilometer.

Notwithstanding its literal creation by gas-powered vehicles, Quartzsite is also relatively ecologically sound. Motorhome dwellers have to live in tight spaces and cut down on waste and, unless they are directly connected to water and power, have to be profoundly conservative about their use of these scarce resources. As a result, Quartzsite is able to subsist on a minimum of infrastructure.

Quartzsite's history reveals how a city can form as an emergent system. Begun as a simple mineral show for desert rock hounds and people passing through the region via highway, it has grown into an instant city, an international travel destination that forms every winter with virtually no top-down planning.

Quartzsite's early history is marked by a series of false starts and brief settlements centered on short-lived stagecoach lines and mines. In 1856, Charles Tyson built Fort Tyson, a private stronghold at a watering hole, for protection against Native Americans. Some nine miles west of the current location of Quartzsite, Tyson's Wells, as the new town came to be known, became a stagecoach station. Of the area in 1874, Martha Summerhayes, author of the 1908 book *Vanished Arizona. Recollections of the Army Life by a New England Woman* would write, "It reeks of everything unclean, morally and physically." [5]

---

[5] Martha Summerhayes, *Vanished Arizona: Recollections of the Army Life by a New England Woman* (Lincoln: University of Nebraska Press, 1979), 134.

Early Quartzsite is best known for its link to a failed military experiment, the United States Camel Corps. The Mexican-American War of 1846-48 made clear to military leaders that securing the rough terrain of the Southwest against Native Americans or the Mexican government, both of whom were unhappy with the growing power of the U. S. in that region, would not be easy. The majority of American causalities in the war in those distant lands fell victim not to enemy fire but to the harsh conditions, proving just how inhospitable that region is to traditional cavalry and infantry.

Convinced they had found a solution, Second Lieutenant George H. Crossman, a veteran of the Seminole Wars and Major Henry C. Wayne, a quartermaster, gained the support of Secretary of War Jefferson Davis and persuaded Congress to allocate $30,000 to create the Camel Military Corps in 1855. Like many such ideas, this seemed sensible at the time. Both Arabia and the American Southwest are similar climatologically. Obviously, dromedaries are well suited to the arid environment and, even if it is hardly plausible that Crossman, Wayne, or Davis would have known this, giant prehistoric camels once roamed the continent. More likely, Crossman and Davis had heard of plans to bring camels to the Mojave desert as pack animals and might even have received word that the animals were being brought to Australia by settlers to help colonize the Outback. In what would be the first operational test of material in the field by the U. S. Army, inaugurating the tradition of operational military research later taken up by General George Owen Squier, the Corps was charged with determining the capabilities of the animals for the possible formation of a camel cavalry, for deployment in artillery units, and for use as pack animals.

Two years later, the Army imported seventy-seven North African camels and a Syrian camel driver named Hadji Ali. Based at Camp Verde, Arizona, some two hundred miles from Quartzsite, the Corps was charged with establishing mail and supply routes westward to California and eastward to Texas.

Although the camels thrived in conditions that would fell any horse, the experiment was not without its problems. The animals did not adapt well to the rocky terrain. They scared other pack animals such as horses and burros. Soldiers found them foul smelling and bad tempered and complained that the camels spat at them. Nevertheless, the new Secretary of War, John Floyd, was impressed and asked Congress for a further 1,000 animals. But tensions between the North and South were rising and the Congress couldn't be bothered with the distant lands of the Southwest. Moreover, upon being appointed Commander of the Texas Army, Major General David E. Twiggs, sometimes known as "The Horse" (but also as "Old Davy" or "the Bengal Tiger") was horrified to discover the Camel Corps in his charge and successfully lobbied Congress to be rid of the beasts. Perhaps it is just as well: Twiggs would soon surrender his command and, with it, the Texas Army to the Confederacy.

Instead of serving the Confederacy, in 1863 the Camel Corps was sold off at auction. Most camels would wind up in private hands, but some would be released into the desert where they became feral. Hadji Ali, now known as "Hi Jolly" remained behind although whether this was to pursue the American dream or simply because he was marooned far from home is unclear. After a time running a camel-borne freight business, Hi Jolly, who was actually half-Greek and also known by the name Philip Tedro, married a Tucson woman and moved to the Tyson's Wells area where he worked as a miner until he died in 1902, reportedly expiring with his arm around one of his camels during a sandstorm. In memory of his service, the government of Arizona built a small pyramid topped by a metal camel to mark his gravesite in the 1930s. Feral camels would be seen roaming the desert until the early 1900s. [6]

For a half century after Hi Jolly's death, the population of Quartzsite remained small, with only about 50 people living in the outpost town on a permanent basis. By the 1950s, however, snowbirds began spending the relatively mild winter months in the area, and by the 1960s the seasonal population could swell to 1,500. Many of these winter travelers returned year-after-year and some settled permanently. As the community slowly grew, businessmen and civic boosters formed the Quartzsite Improvement Association and created a gem and mineral show to encourage more winter travelers to come.

[6] A serviceable history of Quartzsite can be found in Barbara A. Weightman, "The Poor Person's Palm Springs: Quartzsite, Arizona," Donald G. Janelle, ed. *Geographical Snapshot of North America* (New York: Guilford Press, 1992), On the camel corps, see Odie B. Faulk, *The U. S. Camel Corps: an Army Experiment* (Oxford: Oxford University Press, 1976), 346-349.

THE BILBAO EFFECT WITHOUT BUILDINGS

Contemporary urban planners talk of the "Bilbao-effect," suggesting that works of cutting-edge architecture can drive tourists to cities simply through their remarkable appearance, signifying that a city is cool, creative, and de-sign-aware. Quartzsite is like the Bilbao effect, except there are no buildings. Instead there are motorhomes. In retrospect, the development of this self-sufficient beast, capable of hauling a family and enough food and water to sustain it long distances seems almost inevitable.

Mobility has always been a determining aspect of American life. In his 1896 essay "The Significance of the Frontier in American History," Frederick Jackson Turner, the founder of American Studies, observed that until his day United States history had been the product of westward expansion. The presence of the frontier was not just a geopolitical factor. On the con-trary, Turner suggested that it made Americans fundamentally different from Europeans. No matter how rapidly cities on the Atlantic coast ex-panded, he argued, Americans could find a "perennial rebirth" on the fron-tier, "the meeting point between savagery and civilization." Turner wrote poetically of the importance of that thin line between civilization and na-ture to the country:

> The wilderness masters the colonist. It finds him a European in dress, industries, tools, modes of travel, and thought. It takes from him the railroad car and puts him in the birch canoe. It strips off the garments of civilization and arrays him in the hunting shirt and the moccasin. It puts him in the log cabin of the Chero-kee and the Iroquois and runs an Indian palisade around him. Before long he has gone to planting Indian corn and plowing with a sharp stick; he shouts the war cry and takes the scalp in orthodox Indian fashion.

Although the settler eventually transformed the frontier, he too had been transformed. But, Turner concluded, according to the United States Census bureau, the frontier had finally been closed in the 1880s. An epochal shift in the American psyche would follow. [7]

Without the frontier, Americans would have to turn elsewhere. President Teddy Roosevelt urged the country to look for a frontier overseas and began a century-long project of empire building. [8] As the continent was tamed and wild game began to disappear from the American diet, a new regard for wilderness and wildlife emerged. Animal imagery proliferated even as wildlife was domesticated. The fearsome grizzly bear, commonly perceived as a threat to settlers, was replaced in the public imagination by the cute teddy bear, named for Roosevelt after the great sportsman refused to kill an old injured bear that his attendants had lassoed. Roosevelt, an advocate of "the strenuous life," was also instrumental in expanding the National Park System, setting aside by-passed land to remain wilderness in perpetuity, simulating the frontier and thereby allowing Americans to renew themselves as they had before. But if the frontier was a place of production, the perpetual wilderness of the national park is a place of consumption. Nothing can be produced there except the renewal of Americans through recreation. [9]

With the development of the motor car and the National Park System, city dwellers flocked to the countryside for recreation. After Henry Ford built the Model T, his "car for the great multitude," large numbers of individuals fled the city on a regular basis in search of the newly domesticated

[7] Frederick Jackson Turner, *The Frontier in American History* (New York: Henry Holt and Company, 1953), 1-4.

[8] Neil Smith, *American Empire: Roosevelt's Geographer and the Prelude to Globalization* (Berkeley: University of California Press, 2003), 230.

[9] Reuel Denney, *The Astonished Muse* (New Brunswick, NJ: Transaction Publishers, 1989), lxi.

"nature," now freed of grizzly bears, native Americans, and other threats to urban people. Ford himself believed that this would be the Model T's principle use, enabling families to enjoy the blessing of hours of pleasure in God's great open space. Auto camping grew rapidly after World War I. By 1922, the *New York Times* estimated that of 10.8 million cars, 5 million were in use for camping. Soon "auto-tents" and trailers designed to fit the Model T would be available. At first, campers would simply park in empty fields or by the side of the road, but this led to confrontations with angry rural townsfolk, who saw their lives under threat not only from the declining profitability of agriculture but also from the nascent exurbanites they feared would one day gentrify the countryside. In response, campgrounds or "trailer parks" sprang up to provide campers with clearly defined places to stay while on the road. Although campers sought nature and escape from a fixed community, they also enjoyed sharing this experience with their brethren. Unlike the metropolis, trailer parks were places of relative homogeneity—campers were generally middle class whites—so campers were able to tolerate living in remarkably close quarters. During the Depression and Second World War, however, camper trailers acquired a stigma, coming to be used as temporary shelters to be inhabited while their inhabitants worked transient jobs.

By the affluent era of the 1950s, however, Americans once again desired to travel the country in self-sufficient "land yachts," untethered by hotels, inns, or motor courts but the old campers were increasingly unsuitable. Not only did they have the unpleasant connotation of transient housing to overcome, as the sizes of homes grew in suburbia, earlier campers seemed small and cramped. The solution was to integrate the automobile and the trailer, creating the continuous unit now known as the "motorhome" or "Recreational Vehicle." This new kind of vehicle was generally much larger than the campers of old and would permit other activities to

take place while the unit was being driven. Moreover, in doing away with the automobile or truck hauling the camper, the motorhome is clearly a vehicle that cannot be employed for traditional forms of work. You cannot drive your motorhome to a workplace: it exists purely for a lifestyle of leisure and consumption. Outfitted with the latest high technology gadgets such as televisions, tape players, and washing machines, the motorhome echoed the suburban lifestyle. [10]

With the exception of a period during the energy crisis of the 1970s, motorhomes have continued to rise in popularity ever since. Today one in ten American vehicle-owning households owns an RV. But owning a motorhome is a significant commitment demanding time, resources, determination, and the willingness to join a community. Proper maintenance requires specialized skill and a devotion to one's vehicle. The importance of sharing first-hand information about the best campgrounds, motorhome-friendly towns, common repairs and so on leads motorhome dwellers to befriend each other, forming an informal continent-wide network. Motorhome dwellers often gather together in rallies. The biggest such gathering is at Quartzsite.

Since the 1960s, Quartzsite has grown through word-of-mouth in the vast network of motorhome dwellers. Many invite friends to camp with them

[10] Roger B. White, *Home on the Road. The Motor Home in America* (Washington: Smithsonian Institution Press, 2000).

or attend clubs that they are members of. Others, not so well-connected, come to Quartzsite to see what the fuss is about.

At Quartzsite's biggest attraction, the "Main Event" marketplace and showground, a new monument to Hi Jolly and his camel has been built out of automobile rims and mufflers, announcing the fulfillment of the century and a half old vision of self-sufficient desert nomads roaming the West. Riding in their mechanical Camels, these snowbirds ritually re-enact not only the process of settling the frontier, but also their own experience of settling the suburbs, choosing a vacant spot to inhabit next to others just like themselves, thereby recapturing the treasured anonymity and sameness of that era. Since everyone is in a camper, everyone is equal. Pasts are unimportant and incomes matter little. As in the postwar suburb, architecture is alien to Quartzsite. There are different models of motorhome and even some fundamental differences in motorhome typology—the full-fledged land yacht, the persistent trailer, the converted van, the retrofitted bus—and some units may cost $500,000 while others cost $5,000. Nevertheless, a motorhome is a motorhome, a premanufactured unit that is not that dissimilar from other units of its kind. Individual expression is kept to a Protestant minimum. Add a flag, some plastic chairs, even a mat of green Astroturf, but your motorhome is still just about the same as everyone else's and you are, more often than not, five or ten feet away from your neighbor.

The move away from object to communication that occurred alongside the shift from city to suburb is echoed by the social structure designed into campers and motorhomes. Unlike residential architecture, motorhomes are mass produced consumer goods. More alike than McMansions, motorhomes are products with limited consumer options. But unlike automotive design, motorhome design largely eschews fashion or dramatic change. Each year's models vary from those of years past only by recombining the same vocabulary of optional parts and configurations in different ways. Significant change in form or purpose is rare. In addition, the interior of a motorhome is generally fixed, fitted with built-in furnishings and equipment. Sold as a factory interior, the motorhome resists interior decoration and material accumulation, in part due to weight limitations that such vehicles have. The motorhome becomes a capsule for living in a society of networks where changing your location is more important than nesting. Inhabiting a motorhome means embracing life in immaterial culture. The most respected and admired type of motorhome owner is the "full-timer," who has cast off their fixed house permanently in order to dwell nomadically. In the process, the full-timer has to sell virtually all of his or her worldly possessions, abandoning material goods. In the end, the motorhome acts as a kind of animal itself, a modern-day camel, its occupants forming its soul.

Although the motorhome might appear to be an ultimate manifestation of American individualism, just like the trailer campers of the early twentieth century, motorhome owners generally see themselves as part of a community. After all, Quartzsite is the largest gathering of motorhome owners in the nation, assembled purely by the desire to collect together. But this is still a particularly contemporary idea of community. The seventy-odd campsites in Quartzsite are generally privately owned and charge a moderate daily fee for usage. In the private campsite, the motorhome owner does not participate in any governance, choosing to let the "gated community" take care of that. A sizeable percentage of travelers opt out of these areas, "boondocking" on BLM land where it is possible to stay for free for up to two weeks. Campers frequently form small communities on BLM land on the basis of motorhome brand, extended family ties, or group membership. "Birds of a Feather" groups, as they are known, emerge out of common interests. Knappers (individuals skilled in striking pieces of flint with other pieces of flint to make primitive tools and ornaments), HAM radio buffs, Christians, computer fans, Disney lovers, singles, diabetics, full-timers, social nudists, pet lovers, and the Rainbow children (attracted to the freedom of Quartzsite as they wander the country re-creating the hippie lifestyle of the early 1970s) all seek the company of others like themselves at Quartzsite. In this, they reproduce the clustered demographics of posturban America where groups of remarkably specific inhabitants are congealing into discrete communities.

If cities can be treated as communications systems, then they also resemble office environments. During the 1960s, informed by Norbert Wiener's theory of cybernetics, business managers sought means to improve the flow of information in the office and to provide for greater flexibility. Offices, according to this theory, are communications systems. Managers

turned to theories of *Büro Landschaft* or office landscape to replace traditional, rigid-wall offices with more fluid and changeable workplaces. Quartzsite is an urban *Büro Landschaft*. It stands in stark contrast to traditional, gridded cities like Manhattan. Like *Büro Landschaft*, Quartzsite is fluid. Quartzsite allows for divisions between groups to spontaneously occur,
reconfigure at will, and disappear when appropriate. If you don't like your
neighbor or you find that you'd rather be across town, you can just pack up
your motorhome and go. Even though Quartzsite is a city and not an office,
it is truer to the ideals of *Büro Landschaft* than any office could be. Offices
are ultimately based on hierarchy and exploitation. No matter how hard *Büro
Landschaft* tried, it could not hide this. In its purest form, *Büro Landschaft*
would have even have been a form of Communism. At Quartzsite the fact
that few of its winter inhabitants work makes it a much purer model than
any office ever could have been.

WELCOME TO THE HACIENDA

Like the world that Quartzsite is a microcosm of, community at Quartzsite is based on trade. Stimulated by the model of the Quartzsite Improvement Association, nine major gem and mineral shows and more than fifteen general swap meeting shows attract motorhome owners to the area. Much like the young hipsters who populate the fashionable districts of cities like New York, San Francisco, and Los Angeles, campers at Quartzsite generally don't work except as full time consumers. Seemingly incongruous juxtapositions of ever more bizarre goods appear throughout the markets: fresh shrimp cocktails hundreds of miles from the ocean are available next to cow skulls and fox furs dangle near street lights. African sculpture is popular, a demonstration of Quartzsite's role in a global network of nomadic trade. Although there may be variation among the objects for sale, year after year the presence of the market itself draws the migratory residents of Quartzsite back. Ritually appearing and disappearing with the seasons, the marketplace staves off banality and boredom. Barely advertised, it maintains an aura of exclusivity. After wandering for a time at a Quartzsite show like "the Main Event" or the "Tyson Wells Sell-A-Rama," one is gripped by the realization that even the merchants don't come to Quartzsite to make a buck. As more than one sign advertising a vendor's need for a spouse makes clear, merchants are more interested in interacting with people. Some individuals, such as the members of the Hit-and-Miss Engine Show (who restore and demonstrate a particular kind of antique stationary gas engine) discard with the idea of making money altogether, setting up free exhibits instead.

The shopping district at Quartzsite is a critical node for interaction. Closed to motorhome and automotive traffic, the shopping districts serve as the primary conduits for the flow of people and information.

As visitors arrive from around the world and mull over the value of useless objects, they interact in random configurations, thereby sharing knowledge and experiences. With over a million visitors a year, all of these seemingly random conversations carry an enormous amount of information. The interactions remain at a local level, however, and do not generally create any larger direction or impact on the community beyond fostering its perpetual growth.

At Quartzsite, the markets teach us of a new way of life beyond any idea of affluence or material desire. For the most part, the products at Quartzsite's markets are bought and sold to facilitate social relationships, not because they are needed or to establish social status. It's no surprise then, that the central point of Quartzsite's market economy is the exchange of rocks. Often obtained from the surrounding mountains during leisurely hikes and having had minimal labor applied to their retrieval and processing, Quartzsite's rocks circumvent any notion of labor or scarcity in economy. Nor are these rocks useful (or even practical) to the wanderers of the desert. According to Marx, the social character of a producer's labor is only expressed through the exchange of commodities. [11] But there is no labor to speak of in bringing these valueless rocks to sale. Instead of being a source of oppression, as they were in Marx's day, rocks become a source of liberation as they would have been under the never realized Utopian ideal of Communism: "From each according to his abilities, to each according to his needs!" [12]

Like the attendees themselves, the stones of Quartzsite are capable of extreme variation while remaining essentially interchangeable. In writing

[11] Karl Marx and Frederick Engels, *The Communist Manifesto* (London: Verso, 1998), 52.

[12] Karl Marx, "Critique of the Gotha Programme" reprinted in *The Marx-Engels Reader*, ed. Robert C. Tucker (New York: W. W. Norton, 1972), 378-88.

of stones, Roger Caillois has observed "an obvious achievement, yet one arrived at without invention, skill, industry, or anything else that would make it a work in the human sense of the word, much less a work of art. The work comes later, as does art; but the far-off roots and hidden models of both lie in the obscure yet irresistible suggestions in nature." Caillois notes that even when stones are cut and polished, the work involved only reveals something that had always been there. Within these stones, he suggests, we find images, "remarkable likenesses ... regarded as wonders, almost miracles." [13]

Even if they are not works of art, at Quartzsite stones are natural ready-mades, empty of any intrinsic meaning, ready to be filled with abstract signification that can be read, Rorschach-like, out of their random

---

[13] Roger Caillois, *The Writing of the Stones* (Charlottesville: University of Virginia, 1985), 2, 11.

forms. Quartzsite becomes a gallery for the purchase of these objects, which, like works of art, provide meditations on uselessness. Like the ancient festivals of sacrifice, Quartzsite is a place in which the subject can disappear into the system of objects, thereby rejoining the plane of immanence. The exchange of stones is a way for people to remind each other that ultimately theirs is a world in which they are nothing, make nothing, and do not need to labor.

As the capital of the multitude, Quartzsite transgresses capitalism itself to incorporate what were once considered obsolete forms of economy: its market is largely free of capitalism, dwelling is based on feudalism, and individuals, just affluent enough to escape the necessity of labor, are free to pursue their desires, as if under Communism. Markets emerge at Quartzsite in order to facilitate social interaction. At Quartzsite, as in the imagined Hacienda that the Situationists hoped to build, the concept of productive work is obsolete. In place of labor, meaningless exchange is maintained as a form of social interaction.

But Hardt and Negri would be the first to point out that there can be no one capital of the multitude. It is by definition everywhere. So it is with Quartzsite as well. Quartzsite is omnipresent, the id of all horizontal cities. The recent real estate bubble teaches us that houses have no more intrinsic worth than stocks. We dwell in mobile homes sold for fantastic sums bearing no relation to their physical qualities. Just as the dot.com bubble unloaded any meaning from the stock market, the housing bubble has unloaded any meaning from architecture or place. Quartzsite is everywhere today, a transient posturbia absent of any productive capacity, not so much about making money as about enjoying experiences together.

Epilogue

At the onset of this project, we promised that these stories wouldn't add up and, as a collection of extreme conditions, they don't. As we suggested in the introduction, each of these investigations posits a natural philosophy, an autonomous theoretical condition that sometimes appears to mesh with the others but often doesn't.

One day, against of all of our stated intentions, we observed a theme emerging, a common concern with the very problem at the heart of Empire (as well as of religion, the State and other institutions of power): our over-whelming desire to acquiesce and give ourselves up. Invariably, ignoring the admonishments of Nietzsche, designers and theorists assume that power emanates from the top down, that the oppressed individual wants to be free, and that action from the bottom-up is the method for achieving this.

But this is precisely the inverse of what we observe. These stories of humans relentlessly striving to be different only prove their desire for same-ness. So too, in our relationships with objects, collectively we don't so much wish to be free—to escape the world of objects and attachments—but to immerse ourselves within them.

Do we really want freedom? If we can dare to say "maybe not" for a mo-ment, then what do our actions betray about our desires? *Blue Monday* does not offer solutions, instead it suggests that our mass drive to give ourselves up is not a passive action. Instead of condemning this drive (as if we really wanted to or even could) this book offers a collection of stories that just perhaps, hint at another possibility, a first step: self-awareness.

Acknowledgments

Projects in this book were made possible with the support of the Graham Foundation for Advanced Studies in Fine Arts (Ether) as well as the Institute for Multimedia Literacy and the Annenberg Center for Communication, University of Southern California (Swarm Intelligence). Kazys also thanks the Annenberg Center for Communication for the "Networked Publics" fellowship year that allowed him time to complete the book. Many people have helped AUDC and we apologize in advance to anyone we forgot. ACTAR has been a loyal ally throughout and we are delighted to be doing this book with them. 306090's Alex Briseno, Cabinet's Sina Najafi, and Textfield's Jonathan Maghen have been a privilege to publish with. Alex Briseno at Pompeii AD, Kati Rubinyi at Chapman College, Ted Kane at Polarinertia, Fritz Haeg and François Perrin at Art Center College of Design, Mark McManus at the Mountain Bar, Kevin McGarry and Yukie Kamiya at Rhizome as well as Andrea Zittel and Shaun Regen at High Desert Test Sites have graced us with the opportunity to exhibit our work. Matt Coolidge and Sarah Simons not only made possible the pre-AUDC show on One Wilshire at the Center for Land Use Interpretation, they generously offered advice and moral support. David and Diana Wilson at the Museum of Jurassic Technology served as role models for us. Many thanks to John Southern for lending a hand with the Chapman College show and to Steve Rowell for helping install both the show at Chapman and the first High Desert Test Sites show. Jason Buchheit, Jennifer Hurd, Hisako Ichiki, and Jeffrey Kleeger aided us with the Muzak project when it was still in gestation at SCI_Arc. The support and example set by key SCI_Arc faculty, staff, and administration was critical to AUDC, most notably that of Tom Buresh, John Chase, Karl Chu, Christophe Cornubert, Margaret Crawford, Neil Denari, Hernan Diaz-Alonso, Timothy Durfee, Aris Janigian, Perry Kulper, Kevin McMahon, Gary Paige, Margi Reeve, Lisa Russo, Bill Simonian, and Scott Wolfe. Rosalie Genevro and Anne Rieselbach gave us the opportunity to present our work in New York while Vikram Prakash made that possible in Seattle. Criticism from Greg Goldin and Ryan Griffis has been invaluable. Our list of friends, supporters, and individuals who set examples and provided motivation, stimulation, and input over the years includes Steve Anderson, Kadambari Baxi, Julian Bleecker, Denise Bratton, Abbie Chung, Keller Easterling, Frank Escher, Hal Foster, Elaina Ganim and Tim Ventimiglia, Jeffrey Inaba, Mark Jarzombek, Israel Kandarian, Derek Lindner, Megan McEachern, Tara McPherson, Marty McKinney, Lev Manovich, Geoff Manaugh, William Menking, the late Rose Mendez, William Mohline, Valdas Ožarinskas, Scott Rigby, Nick Roberts, Mark Shepard, Paulette Singley, Stephanie Smith, Marc Tuters, Geoffrey Waite and Mimi Zeiger. Kazys owes immense gratitude to Mark Wigley for providing the ideal environment in which to finish the book. Special thanks to Reinhold Martin. Undying gratitude to Nikki Burt and Esmeralda Ward for all of their help throughout the years, especially in the days leading up to the opening of the Wilshire Boulevard facility. Above all, Kazys wishes to thank Jennifer, Liam, Viltis, and Daisy for their patience and love during the lengthy gestation of this project and both of us thank our parents and families for making this possible.

Published by
Actar
www.actar.com
info@actar.com

Author
AUDC
www.audc.org
Robert Sumrell and Kazys Varnelis
www.robertsumrell.com and www.varnelis.net

Preface
Reinhold Martin

Graphic Design
Lea

Printing
Ingoprint S.A.

Distribution
Actar D
Roca i Batlle 2
E-08023 Barcelona
Tel +34 934174993
Fax +34 934186707
office@actar-d.com
www.actar-d.com

Distribution in the United States
Actar Distribution Inc
158 Lafayette St. 5th Floor
New York, NY 10013
Tel +1 212 966 2207
Fax +1 212 966 2214
officeusa@actar-d.com
www.actar-d.com

ISBN **978-84-96540-53-8**
DL **B-26109-2006**

Printed and bound in the European Union

Other titles in the collection, Catherine Spellman,
Re-envisioning Landscape/Architecture (ISBN 84-95273-99-3)
Actar, Barcelona 2003